There Is No Such thing As Hate Speech:

A Case for Absolute Freedom of Expression

There Is No Such thing As Hate Speech:

A Case for Absolute Freedom of Expression

by
Ravi Shanker Kapoor

BLOOMSBURY
NEW DELHI • LONDON • OXFORD • NEW YORK • SYDNEY

First published in India 2017
This export edition published in 2020

ISBN: 978-93-86432-72-8

Bloomsbury Publishing India Pvt. Ltd
Second Floor, LSC Building No.4
DDA Complex, Pocket C – 6 & 7, Vasant Kunj
New Delhi 110070
www.bloomsbury.com

Typeset by Manipal Digital Systems

Dedication

This book is dedicated to my elder brother and mentor,
Late Sh. Gauri Shanker Kapoor.

Contents

Dedication		v
Preface		ix
Lemma		xi
Chapter 1	Freedom of expression = Right to offend, right to blaspheme	1
Chapter 2	Freedom of expression in independent India	11
Chapter 3	First Amendment: American and Indian	14
Chapter 4	The Left and the Right of freedom	20
Chapter 5	Expression versus Law & Order	24
Chapter 6	How censor board and others torment filmmakers	32
Chapter 7	Film censorship and the law of inexorability	40
Chapter 8	Nannies and grannies of all ages	45
Chapter 9	Hurting the sentiments-I	49
Chapter 10	Hurting the sentiments-II	53
Chapter 11	Freedom and science are inseparable	58
Chapter 12	Freedom and faith	67
Chapter 13	Script for political correctness	73
Chapter 14	Doublespeak by liberals	81

Chapter 15	The defamation bugbear	84
Chapter 16	In love with chains	88
Chapter 17	The cartoonish controversies	91
Chapter 18	Suppositions galore	95
Chapter 19	What really encourages rioters	99
Chapter 20	'World-class freedom'	105
Chapter 21	Ban on pornography is illiberal	109
Chapter 22	The permanence of Section 66A	116
Chapter 23	What West does and what we do when freedom is under fire	123
Chapter 24	Internet censorship: A growing menace	133
Chapter 25	Global threats to liberty	136
Chapter 26	There no such thing as hate speech	142
About The Author		147

Preface

There are debates all over the world as to what constitutes hate speech, when does one cross the line, how to protect freedom of expression while checking hate speech, and so on. Several writers and thinkers have expressed their opinions on the subject, and many have offered scholarly arguments to bolster the cause of liberty. Yet, I think that the issue has not been studied in a comprehensive manner. *There Is No Such Thing As Hate Speech: A Case for Absolute Freedom of Expression* is an attempt to fill that void.

The book takes into account the philosophical background of the subject; it delves into such relationships as freedom and science, freedom and faith, and freedom versus Law & Order; it discusses issues like pornography, censorship, and defamation; the book also lists the multifarious threats to liberty and their growing virulence. At the risk of sounding immodest, I would like to say that the book provides a 360-degree view of the subject.

As evident from the subtitle, the book presents an absolutist position: freedom of expression has to be absolute, without any restraints, otherwise it is not freedom. It should be regulated only by the Harm Principle: that is, expression should be punished only if it leads to imminent harm to somebody. Mine is an extreme position but, as American conservative statesman Barry Goldwater said, 'Extremism in the defense of liberty is no vice. And moderation in the pursuit of justice is no virtue.'

Before building up my case, I have examined nationalism in general and Indian nationalism in particular. My view is that Indians should outgrow nationalism, a modern pathology, and embrace the ideas and ideals of the Enlightenment. This essay is a lemma to the thesis that unrestrained freedom is the prerequisite of meaningful human existence. Whether or not I am able to convincingly argue my case is for the reader to judge.

Lemma

Poverty of Indian nationalism

Nationalism is hunger for power tempered by self-deception. Every nationalist is capable of the most flagrant dishonesty, but he is also—since he is conscious of serving something bigger than himself—unshakably certain of being in the right. George Orwell

That British rule was an unmitigated disaster is an axiomatic truth for almost all Indians. Politicians and intellectuals of all persuasions—from communists and socialists to Gandhians, Nehruvians, and Hindu nationalists—are unanimous in averring that the Raj was anunmixed evil. Its end is celebrated at the national level. Few, if any, have dared to challenge the validity and indubitableness of the axiom. It is time we did that.

15 August 1947 is Independence Day. Before that, the Union Jack flew over India. We were governed by the inhabitants of a distant island nation, according to the rules made by them to suit their purposes. It ended that day; we became free of foreign domination; we ceased to be dependent upon them; we became Independent. This is the nationalist narrative.

This is not to say that the narrative is completely false. Yes, the British framed laws to largely further their own objectives; they set up institutions to perpetuate the Empire; they promoted the land revenue system to bolster the exchequer; they framed economic policy that bolstered the manufacturers of Manchester and Lancashire rather than those of Kanpur and Bombay; they created an administration to suppress and repress the natives rather than 'organise liberty with order'; they established the police that had least regard for human rights; in almost everything they did, the interests of their mother country preceded those of the colony. Yet, I would like to emphasise that their predecessors were infinitely worse than them, for the history of Muslim rule in India is the history of massacres, genocide, destruction, benightedness, rape, rapine, and rapacity. In comparison, the British—despite the avarice of Clive, the expansionism of Dalhousie, the haughtiness of Lytton, the arrogance of Curzon, and the brutality of General Dyer—were angels.

More importantly, the British were no worse than their successors.

We, the people of India, have failed to appreciate a simple fact: rulers usually are either bad or very bad. Such lack of cognition has happened—as we shall see in the following pages—primarily because we have unquestionably accepted and mindlessly internalised the idea that government and only government is the prime mover in any society. The British, our nationalists believed, were responsible for the poverty, backwardness, and other problems. If only we could have a good—that is, nationalist—government, everything will be taken care of. Therefore, India's Independence was of paramount importance. Or so we were told.

Back in 1917, in his book *Nationalism*, Rabindranath Tagore had anticipated the flaw in Indian nationalist thinking:

> The general opinion of the majority of the present-day nationalists in India is that we have come to a final completeness in our social and spiritual ideals, the task of the constructive work of society having been done several thousand years before we were born, and that now we are free to employ all our activities in the political direction. We never dream of blaming our social inadequacy as the origin of our present helplessness, for we have accepted as the creed of our nationalism that this social system has been perfected for all time to come by our ancestors, who had the superhuman vision of all eternity and supernatural power for making infinite provision for future ages. Therefore, for all our miseries and shortcomings, we hold responsible the historical surprises that burst upon us from outside. This is the reason why we think that our one task is to build a political miracle of freedom upon the quicksand of social slavery.

Blinding power of nationalism

Notice the blinding, maddening power of nationalism. At a time when ills of every kind afflicted our society, when women were treated like cattle, education was sparse and superstition rampant, our nationalists were convinced about the 'final completeness in our social and spiritual ideals'! Nationalism blinded us—still blinds us; we are unable or unwilling to see that India's rendezvous with the West was most beneficent in the history of our country, for it was this meeting that brought the great Enlightenment ideas of liberty and reason to the Indian shores, even though the carriers of these ideas were not the most enlightened souls; indeed, many of them were crooks and scoundrels.

Merriam-Webster defines nationalism as 'a feeling that people have of being loyal to and proud of their country, often with the belief that it is better and more important than other countries.' Further, it is 'a desire by a large group of people (such as people who share the same culture, history, language, etc.) to form a separate and independent nation of their own.'

The feeling and the desire, even with a little bit of pride, may not be dangerous. In India however, nationalists went over the top, almost right from the beginning—that is, when patriotism transmogrified into nationalism around the turn of the century. The self-critical glance of the nineteenth century socio-religious reforms was replaced with the anti-British proclivities and then jingoistic fervour. They started blaming the imperial rulers for all of our problems; instead of reforming and rejuvenating the society from within, we began imbibing the tenets of nationalism. We turned our backs on what was the best in the West—liberalism, rationalism, individualism, limited government, *et al.* And we developed a penchant for Western diseases—nationalism, socialism, fascism. As Tagore wrote, 'we want to dam up the true course of our own historical stream, and only borrow power from the sources of other peoples' history.'

India's historical stream had been effectively dammed up by the gates of nationalism—the stream had got a fresh charge of life with the arrival of the British. They came here as traders and then became rulers. It was an encounter of epic proportions. India had been defeated many times before that—the Greeks, the Kushans, the Shakas, the Huns, the Muslims. But almost always the conquerors were conquered by the culture, ethos, and easy *modus vivendi* of the vanquished; most of the victorious tribes ended up as becoming a caste or a community, getting absorbed into Hinduism. Even the Muslims, with their exclusivist religion and their almost uninterrupted 600-year rule, developed an Indian identity, though it was not monolithic. In general, in the northern and north-western parts, India was Islamised—with the Hindus adopting the language, culture, and manners of Muslims. However, in eastern and southern areas, Islam was Indianised—with the Muslims speaking Bengali, Malayalam, *etc.*, and adopting Hindu manners.

The Muslim conquest, however, did not fundamentally change the Hindu. Hindu society, facing the onslaught of Islam, did not reform itself much; rather, historians tell us that caste rules often became stricter, and in general social restrictions intensified. There were also more restrictions on sea voyage and certain economic activities such as agriculture were disparaged.

There was the Bhakti or Devotion Movement (800 AD to 1,700 AD) in the medieval period. As the name suggests, it was a Hindu religious movement in which devotion to God was the principal spiritual practice for the attainment of salvation. With its origins in South India, it gradually spread to the north. It was a popular movement which often enjoyed the sanction of great philosophers and the patronage of royalty. The great saints and poets wrote passionately against the rigidities of Brahminical orthodoxy and helped mitigate the severities of the social system.

Yet, despite its essentially humanitarian message, it was not an intellectual movement; it was not even a shadow of the Renaissance or the Enlightenment. No questions about the individual and his role in society were ever asked; the relationship between the individual and the state was rarely discussed; human freedom was never expressed in secular terms. If at all, liberty and the human condition were the concern for, in the words of Isaiah Berlin, a 'retreat into an inner citadel,' a yearning for the '*noumenal* self.' In fact, it was an insidiously anti-intellectual movement, for its soothing, humane temperament lulled men and women to seek solace in the flights of divine fancies and in the labyrinths of mythological splendours. The Devotional Movement was indeed, to use Marx's words, an 'opiate of the masses.'

The beginning of the nineteenth century saw the consolidation of British power in India. This brought the two civilisations, the Indian and the Western, face to face. Interestingly, the civilisational rendezvous did not begin with a clash, despite the background of decades-old political and military conflicts between the two sides, and the righteous indignation expressed by the Christian missionaries about the pagan darkness prevalent in the country. The result was the phenomenon of Orientalism—I use the term in an ideology-neutral sense, without Edward Said's baggage.

Indian historians of almost all persuasions view Orientalism as the product and function of the needs of the East India Company (this is essentially a nationalist assumption which I do not agree with). The Company, we are told, wanted to know what India was all about. Warren Hastings, the first Governor-General of India (1773-1785) said, 'To rule effectively, one must love India; to love India, one must communicate with her people; to communicate with her people, one must acquire her languages.'

When India was the East

It is important to remember that for the Western mind, India was the East. The entire geopolitical nomenclature involving the word 'East' is oriented around the concept of India being the East. The Near East is what is near to the West, which was Europe till the New World was discovered and colonised; the Middle East was a little farther; the Far East was the farthest outpost of mankind.

More than any other country or civilisation, it was India which had excited, roused, and stirred the scholars and adventurers. The Middle East was not much unfamiliar; its prominent religion Islam was after all Semitic in origin and therefore, cognate to Christianity. The West had an antagonistic relation with Islam, with hostilities going back to the pre-Crusades period and the problems with the Ottoman Turks in later centuries. The Far East was too distant. For the West, it was India that was exotic, rich, and full of marvels. Vasco da Gama and Columbus undertook hazardous voyages to reach India. Yet, despite curiosity about India, not much was known about it. That was why, the Orientalists—fired by the Enlightenment ideals of humanism, rationalism, and classicism, and supported by the newly established colonial authority—began their studies in philology, archeology, history, and Indian classics in the 1770s.

Governor-General Wellesley set up the College of Fort William in 1800. It emerged as the major centre of Orientalism in India. A big library was founded; books were published in not only the classical languages, Sanskrit and Persian, but also in Bengali, Marathi, Urdu, and Hindi.

Sanskrit and Persian scholars were engaged. The college translated and published more than one hundred Sanskrit texts.

These developments introduced India not only to the West but also to the Indians for the first time in recorded history. Bengal's elite acquired knowledge about the country's past and imbibed many Enlightenment ideals; hence the Bengal Renaissance. In this context, it is pertinent to distinguish the thinking and feeling of the leading lights of the Bengal Renaissance like Raja Rammohun Roy and Ishwarchand Vidyasagar from those of the nationalists of the late nineteenth andtwentieth centuries. The former were inspired by patriotism—the love of one's country—and wanted modernisation and progress; in this endeavour, they wanted the British to play a key role. In contradistinction to this, the primary goal of later nationalists was to oustthe British.

First to get acquainted with the progress made by the West, the early patriots were acutely conscious of the rot that had set in every aspect of their own country—political, social, cultural, philosophical, scientific, and technological. In the early nineteenth century, Britain (representing the West) was making great strides. The political system was well in place and properly functioning: its navy ruled the waves; its army was defeating or subduing prince-after-dissolute-prince; its economy was booming, thanks to the Industrial Revolution which was in full swing.

Western philosophy—Burke, John Stuart Mill, Voltaire, Rousseau, *et al*—reached the Indian shores as a breath of fresh air, enlivening and invigorating the climate of opinion. It was not that philosophers did not exist in India before the advent of the British. In fact, the profundity of all the streams of Indian philosophy impressed many Orientalists and, especially, the metaphysically-sophisticated Germans. Unsurprisingly, the leading Indologist Max Mueller—after whom a road is named in New Delhi—was German. Schopenhauer was influenced by Indian thought.

Yet, the Indian philosophical tradition—profound and abstruse though it was—could never break free of recondite metaphysics and nerve-wrecking epistemology; it had little, if any, relationship with public life or politics. For instance, the classical six schools of Indian philosophy scarcely ever touched the issues such as the relation between the individual and the state, the plight of Shudras, and the morality or rationality of inhuman practices like suttee. Against this backdrop, the imported ideas of liberty, equality, humanism, individual's rights, and limited government metamorphosed several generations of Indians.

The metamorphosis

The metamorphosis made them see India in a way that was different from the perspective of their ancestors. They were moved by and enraged with the barbarous practices like suttee, the dehumanisation of the lower strata of society, the inhuman caste rules, and other social rigidities. It was the love for their country that aroused and galvanised them to launch various social and religious reform movements.

The seeds of nationalism, which grew in vehemence later, were sown at the time when the British finalised the contours of the education system in India. Thomas Babington Macaulay, the British poet and historian, was Secretary to the Board of Control from 1832 until 1833. After the Government of India Act 1833 was passed, he became the first Law Member of the Governor-General's Council. He came to India in 1834 and between 1834 and 1838, served at the Supreme Council of India. Apart from drafting the Indian Penal Code in the 1850s, he chalked out the modern education system by convincing the Governor-General and others to adopt English, rather than Sanskrit or Arabic, as the medium of instruction in higher education, from the sixth year of schooling onwards. In his famous (or infamous) 'Minute of 2 February 1835 on Indian Education,' he wrote:

> We must at present do our best to form a class who may be interpreters between us and the millions whom we govern; a class of persons, Indian in blood and colour, but English in taste, in opinions, in morals, and in intellect.

This 43-word sentence from a minute containing about 5,500 words is often quoted to substantiate the thesis that the British, after militarily conquering India, launched the enterprise to vanquish it culturally, ideologically, and spiritually; that they wanted to obliterate Indian civilisation. Worse, they wanted to use a section of Indians in this vile venture; they sought to transmogrify a class of Indians and use them to rule the country.

The fact, however, is that Macaulay's intentions were admirable. He wanted the Enlightenment to reach India and help the Indians lead a good life. He wanted the Indians—at any rate, a section of Indians—to be familiar with the best that the West could offer. He wanted them to be familiar with science, history, literature, and other modern subjects for material and intellectual progress. He did exhibit European arrogance when he said that:

> ...all the historical information which has been collected from all the books written in the Sanscrit language is less valuable than what may be found in the most paltry abridgments used at preparatory schools in England. In every branch of physical or moral philosophy, the relative position of the two nations is nearly the same... I have never found one among them who could deny that a single shelf of a good European library was worth the whole native literature of India and Arabia.

But this arrogance was not without grounds, as the traditional scholarly pursuits in those days were little more than an exercise in barren intellectualism and pedantic speculation. Conventional scholarship was ignorant of the scientific and geographical developments of the previous few centuries; it was nothing but semantic hair-splitting. It was against this background that Macaulay wrote:

> There are in modern times, to go no further, two memorable instances of a great impulse given to the mind of a whole society, —of prejudices overthrown, —of knowledge diffused, —taste purified, —of arts and sciences planted in countries which had recently been ignorant and barbarous.
>
> The first instance to which I refer, is the great revival of letters among the Western nations at the close of the fifteenth and the beginning of the sixteenth centuries. At that time almost every thing that was worth reading was contained in the writings of the ancient Greeks and Romans. Had our ancestors acted as the Committee of Public Instruction has hitherto acted; had they neglected the language of Cicero and Tacitus; had they confined their attention to the old dialects of our own island; had they printed nothing and taught nothing at the universities but Chronicles in Anglo-Saxon, and Romances in Norman-French, would England have been what she now is? What the Greek and Latin were to the contemporaries of More and

Ascham, our tongue is to the people of India. The literature of England is now more valuable than that of classical antiquity. I doubt whether the Sanscrit literature be as valuable as that of our Saxon and Norman progenitors. In some departments, —in History, for example, I am certain that it is much less so.

Another instance may be said to be still before our eyes. Within the last hundred and twenty years, a nation which has previously been in a state as barbarous as that in which our ancestors were before the crusades, has gradually emerged from the ignorance in which it was sunk, and has taken its place among civilised communities—I speak of Russia. There is now in that country a large educated class, abounding with persons fit to serve the state in the highest functions, and in no wise inferior to the most accomplished men who adorn the best circles of Paris and London. There is reason to hope that this vast empire, which in the time of our grandfathers was probably behind the Punjab, may, in the time of our grandchildren, be pressing close on France and Britain in the career of improvement. And how was this change effected? Not by flattering national prejudices: not by feeding the mind of the young Muscovite with the old women's stories which his rude fathers had believed; not by filling his head with lying legends about St. Nicholas: not by encouraging him to study the great question, whether the world was or was not created on the 13th of September not by calling him 'a learned native,' when he has mastered all these points of knowledge: but by teaching him those foreign languages in which the greatest mass of information had been laid up, and thus putting all that information within his reach. The languages of Western Europe civilised Russia. I cannot doubt that they will do for the Hindoo what they have done for the Tartar.

Macaulay vindicated

This is true. Macaulay's insistence on English proved to be correct even after the British had left India. Many linguistic fanatics sought to promote vernaculars at the expense of English, and this has had deplorable consequences; it has created a new caste system, with the higher caste comprising those proficient in English and the lower one with people who do not know much about it. It is a typical instance of oriental hypocrisy: the politicians who vociferously championed the cause of vernaculars sent their own children to English-medium schools, thus equipping them to thrive in the real world; but their policies meant that the ordinary people, who relied on government schools, could not offer proper education in English.

On the whole, almost all Indians have viewed Macaulay's insistence on the English language and his project of civilisational engineering—forming 'a class of persons, Indian in blood and colour, but English in taste, in opinions, in morals, and in intellect'—as evidence of the wicked imperial design to subjugate India, the design whose integral part was the production of clerks and lower-level officials to perpetuate the Raj. This essentially nationalist theory overlooks or obscures two important facts. First, Macaulay wanted to promote the universal, Enlightenment ideals, which most Indians, over the years, started viewing as a set of British ideals devised by the imperialists. Macaulay's impatience with oriental mumbo-jumbo, especially the 'extravagantly absurd' Hindu religion, did not endear him to the nationalists.

Second, Macaulay did what was desired by Raja Rammohon Roy, the noblest and most open-minded Indian of the first half of the nineteenth century. On 11 December1823—that is, twelve years before Macaulay wrote his famous Minute, Roy opposed the decision to set up a new Sanskrit school in Calcutta. In his petition to William Pitt, he wrote:

> We understood that the Government in England had ordered a considerable sum of money to be annually devoted to the instruction of its Indian Subjects. We were filled with sanguine hopes that this sum would be laid out in employing European Gentlemen of talents and education to instruct the natives of India in Mathematics, Natural Philosophy, Chemistry, Anatomy and other useful Sciences, which the Nations of Europe have carried to a degree of perfection that has raised them above the inhabitants of other parts of the world.

We already offered up thanks to Providence for inspiring the most generous and enlightened of the Nations of the West with the glorious ambitions of planting in Asia the Arts and Sciences of modern Europe…

[But] we now find that the Government are establishing a Sangscrit school under Hindoo Pundits to impart such knowledge as is already current in India. This Seminary (similar in character to those which existed in Europe before the time of Lord Bacon) can only be expected to load the minds of youth with grammatical niceties and metaphysical distinctions of little or no practicable use to the possessors or to society. The pupils will there acquire what was known two thousand years ago, with the addition of vain and empty subtleties since produced by speculative men, such as is already commonly taught in all parts of India.

The Sangscrit language, so difficult that almost a lifetime is necessary for its perfect acquisition, is well-known to have been for ages a lamentable check on the diffusion of knowledge.

...the Sangscrit system of education would be the best calculated to keep this country in darkness.

Was Raja Rammohon Roy also a tool of the British?

A couple of remarks need to be made at this juncture. First, what brought disrepute to the Macaulayan project was not its supposed immorality and malevolence, but the imperialist imperative; it was the gulf between the ideals of the project and the racist arrogance of the British, especially after the advent of nationalism in India. Over the decades, the mistrust between the British and Indians grew in intensity. From the mid-nineteenth century onwards, especially after the Revolt in 1857, many British officials disliked the Indianisation of civil service.

Their resentment found expression in their opposition to the Ilbert Bill. The 1883 legislation proposed by the Viceroy, Lord Ripon, would allow Indian judges and magistrates the jurisdiction to try British offenders in criminal cases at the district level. The Bill evoked loud, racist protests from the British, particularly British tea and indigo plantation owners in Bengal.

Ironically, the class which Macaulay and earlier imperialists wanted to create 'who may be interpreters between us and the millions whom we govern' came to harbour the bitterest feelings against the Empire. In fact, it was this class which started expressing dissent over various issues (and which eventually ended the Raj). Further, being the buffer between the British and Indians, the spiritual progeny of Macaulay bore the brunt of imperial superciliousness and racial discrimination. It is not surprising that the earliest issue raised by this class was related to government jobs, especially civil services. Consider the case of Sir Surendranath Banerjea who came from a distinguished (*kulin*) family of Brahmins. After college education, he applied in England to enter the Indian Civil Service. But his case was rejected on the ground of misrepresentation of age. Banerjea however, won his appeal. He was sent to Sylhet, now in Bangladesh, but was dismissed in 1874. The entire episode of his appointment and dismissal caused considerable clamour in the genteel society (*bhadralok*) of Bengal. It proved to be a landmark in India's modern history (Banerjea embarked on a teaching career for the next thirty-seven years. He became an active public and political figure. He set up associations; he became president of the Indian National Congress twice).

Men like Banerjea, who were members of the nascent middle class, increasingly suffered the slights hurled at them by the British. Meanwhile they were also organising themselves in modern ways: they were setting up associations, organising meetings, analysing and sometimes criticising official policies, petitioning the authorities to carry out or expedite social reforms, publishing newspapers and magazines, printing pamphlets.

By their work, the early patriots prepared the ground for nationalism. While patriotism is simply love for one's country, nationalism—being love for one's nation—is quite complex. First, the term 'nation' is never without ambiguity. What defines a nation—race, ethnicity, creed, language, culture (but then what is culture?), or a permutation or combination of all these? There is no clarity or consensus among scholars. Patriotism, on the other hand, is much simpler, being firmly rooted in land—even literally, as it is derived from the Latin 'patris' or father; hence the term 'fatherland'. Patriotism is spontaneous, often inarticulate; nationalism is well-thought out and passionately reasoned. Patriotism is; nationalism argues.

Patriotism versus nationalism

I will give an illustration. If there is a calamity—earthquake, flood, *etc.*—the patriotic response is simple and unambiguous: 'Do whatever to save lives.' That would include help from other countries. The nationalist response, however, would be complicated and cautious; there would be diffidence, even reluctance, to seek help from other countries. How would this reflect on us; can't a great nation like ours solve our own problems—this is how the nationalist mind works. National glory is more important than human life, for the nation is much more than the sum total of nationals. This happened in the wake of the Gujarat earthquake of 2002: the Indian Government got but did not *seek* foreign help from others—at least, that was the official position.

This brings us to the more important difference between patriotism and nationalism; it pertains to defining and building a nation. In this process, undue glorification—that is, attaching fictitious attributes to, or embellishing and amplifying the attributes of, economic classes, social groups, occupations, and policies—plays the most substantive role. Imaginary qualities are attributed to some theoretical construct. Mythologies are conjured up to suit the political and ideological objectives; history is moulded or distorted to suit the interests of the political class; fairy tales fashion folklore with national leitmotifs; truths, half-truths, and untruths blend to prepare a concoction to the liking of the collective psyche of a people. This is what glorification does.

Even before the Enlightenment project could mature, before the Indians could fully imbibe the ideals of individual liberty and reason, before liberty could be harmonised with order, before the concept of limited government could be properly comprehended, the nationalism enterprise found a firm footing. It was mainly an exercise in asserting national self-esteem, which was frequently wounded by the haughtiness of the British.

In the eyes of the educated Indians, the British were far ahead of us in all aspects but one: the spiritual. As we noticed earlier, it was only in the realm of metaphysical speculation that India could boast of some depth—and even the Orientalists recognised this. It was this aspect which was concentrated upon and magnified by nationalists. In an address in 1897, Swami Vivekanand said:

> Let others talk of politics, of the glory of acquisition of immense wealth poured in by trade, of the power and spread of commercialism, of the glorious fountain of physical liberty; but these the Hindu mind does not understand and does not want to understand. Touch him on spirituality, on religion, on God, on the soul, on the Infinite, on spiritual freedom, and I assure you, the lowest peasant in India is better informed on these subjects than many a so-called philosopher in other lands. I have said, gentlemen, that we have yet something to teach to the world. This is the very reason, the *raison d'etre*, that this nation has lived on, in spite of hundreds of years of persecution, in spite of foreign rule and foreign oppression. This nation still lives; the *raison d'etre* still holds to God, to the treasure-house of religion and spirituality.

Notice the stupendous glorification: the great saint endows the Hindu mind with all the glories of spirituality, almost completely overlooking the corruptions in Hindu society. When he spoke these words, millions of Hindus, the untouchables, lived a subhuman existence; many of them were bound by tradition to carry human excreta. A mere touch of these unfortunate people was considered polluting for caste Hindus. There was scarcely any education for women; most of them were married at an early age, child marriage being the norm; the mores of 'the treasure-house of religion and spirituality' granted them few legal rights. Yet, the Swami sang of the eternal splendours of Hinduism:

> In this land are, still, religion and spirituality, the fountains which will have to overflow and flood the world to bring in new life and new vitality to the Western and other nations, which are now almost borne down, half-killed, and degraded by political ambitions and social scheming.

Such discourses gave rise to the Indian spiritualism-Western materialism dichotomy. The dichotomy went on to shape Indian nationalism. Collective conceit played a major role in the shaping up of nationalism. It always plays an important role in fashioning any nationalism; sometimes, the consequences are apocalyptic, e.g., in Germany. In India, the result was not jingoistic aggression, but a closing up of the mind.

Nationalist pride acquired mythological proportions. Many Indians started claiming—and they still do—that several of the modern wonders like airplanes and missiles were known to our ancestors. What else was Pushpak Vimaan(a flying machine mentioned in Hindu scriptures); what were the devastating firearms mentioned in the *Mahabharata*, they ask. Even in this day and age, such fascination for pseudo-science is rampant. 'We can feel proud of what our country achieved in medical science at one point of time,' Prime Minister Narendra Modi told a gathering of doctors and other professionals at a hospital in Mumbai in October 2014. 'We all read about Karna in the *Mahabharata*. If we think a little more, we realise that the *Mahabharata* says Karna was not born from his mother's womb. This means that genetic science was present at that time. That is why Karna could be born outside his mother's womb.'

Plastic surgery and organ transplantation was also there: 'We worship Lord Ganesha. There must have been some plastic surgeon at that time who got an elephant's head on the body of a human being and began the practice of plastic surgery.'

The Indian Prime Minister also discussed the contributions of 'people like Aryabhata (476-550)', the mathematician-astronomer whose achievements are universally accepted. That is a big problem: pseudo-science piggybacks science. As Nirad C. Chaudhuri wrote in *The Autobiography of an Unknown Indian*:

> Towards the end of the [nineteenth] century the Hindu counter-reformation swung to the opposite pole of grotesqueness. From late Sanskrit scholasticism it passed to scientific claptrap. Every Hindu custom and every Hindu taboo found its justification in some theory of electricity and magnetism. At times even the science of bacteriology, new at the time, was invoked. It was proclaimed that if a Hindu kept a pigtail it was only as an electromagnetic coil; if he bathed in the Ganges it was because an unspecified European (preferably a German) scientist had demonstrated that Ganges water killed bacteria instantaneously; if he fasted at full and new moon it was only to counteract the gravitational forces of the sun and the moon; the Diwali illumination was supposed to be collective lighting of fire for burning up the poisonous gases given off by the earth on that evening.

So, science did not triumph over superstition; rather, the former bolstered the latter in many cases. Against this backdrop, the weakening of the social reform spirit and the concomitant resurrection of rot in Hindu society were not surprising developments. The desire to look inwards—to detect the shortcomings in society, its moorings, and values—weakened. One of the results, therefore, was a false sense of self-sufficiency: yes, there are problems in our society, but we are capable of tackling them. Long before Jawaharlal Nehru led the nation on the path of self-sufficiency and self-reliance in the sphere of economy, resulting in entropy, nationalists started viewing social evils in the national perspective: only we can take care of our society; the British should steer clear of it.

In any case, the biggest problem, in the eyes of nationalists, was not social but political: indeed British rule *was* the problem. Important people of India had stopped looking inwards; they were not scrutinising, debating, or critiquing their own society, culture, mores, and values; they had found an enemy to fight with—and to criticise for every affliction that affected us. Tagore was an honourable exception, though. He said: 'Our real problem in India is not political. It is social.'

Intolerant nationalism

Criticisms by others were also dismissed with remarkable cantankerousness. For example, when Katherine Mayo wrote a scathing book, *Mother India*, the Indians were enraged. Even Mahatma Gandhi called it a 'drain inspector's report.' It was a typical response: we were unwilling to take criticism in the right spirit, especially from an outsider. This was true nationalism—my country, right or wrong.

It was because of such a national mood that the enemy, the British Empire, was maligned and blamed for all the ills of the nation. And since we had convinced ourselves that British rule was responsible for all ills, its abolition would mean the end, or the beginning of the end of all problems.

Gradually, as the nationalist movement gathered steam with the strengthening of the Indian National Congress, social reforms were sucked into it. Under Mahatma Gandhi's stewardship, they became an integral but minor part of the nationalist movement. The Enlightenment project took the backseat; few talked about individual liberty, open society, limited government, *etc*; the nation was of paramount interest. For Congress leaders and members in the 1920s, 1930s, and 1940s, national freedom became the overriding concern.

It was against this backdrop that Subhas Chandra Bose (1897-1945) came into prominence. He was the worst tyrant we never had (though most Indians adore this admirer of Hitler and Mussolini, and think that his untimely death was one of the most tragic events for the nation in the twentieth century). In Bose, the pathology of nationalism reached its zenith and almost touched Fascism and Nazism. His blind and rabid nationalism made him the greatest enemy of the core Enlightenment ideals in India in his time. In his inaugural speech as mayor of Calcutta in 1930, he spoke about 'a synthesis' of '[s]ocialism and Fascism. We have here the justice, the equality, the love, which is the basis of Socialism, and combined with that we have the efficiency and the discipline of Fascism as it stands in Europe today.'

It was not a young man's fascination for the two violent collectivist ideologies; it was a typical twentieth century Big Brother's preamble for a Gulag that, luckily, never came into being. He worked hard for the great synthesis. In 1944, addressing students at Tokyo University, he favoured a political system 'of an authoritarian character/...\To repeat once again, our philosophy should be a synthesis between National Socialism and communism.'

A perennial adolescent, he could never get rid of his admiration for the meretricious attainments of Fascist Italy and Nazi Germany; he was mesmerised by the apparent order, discipline, unity, and efficiency in totalitarian countries. He was also inspired by the personality cult that grew around the tyrants Hitler and Mussolini; when Bose organised his ragtag outfit (grandiloquently named the Indian National Army) of deserters from the British Indian Army, he even got the chance to imitate his heroes—replete with military uniform, peak cap, knee-length boots, *et al.* Even before donning the mantle of national liberator, and still part of the staid Congress, he showed great predilection for pomp and personal glory. At the fifty-first session of the Congress party at Haripura in 1938, where he had been elected party president, Bose's entry was spectacular. He was escorted by fifty-one girls in saffron saris; his chariot was pulled by fifty-one white bullocks; the two-hour procession passed through fifty-one specially-constructed gates; there were fifty-one brass bands. He anticipated Narendra Modi in terms of pomp and pageant.

As with many twentieth century dictators, he also had an epithet, Netaji, or 'revered leader.' Bose clearly encouraged the use of Netaji. His entire life was a crusade against the most cherished Enlightenment concept: individual liberty. In 1935, he wrote:

> One is inclined to hold that the next phase in world-history will produce a synthesis between Communism and Fascism. And will it be a surprise if that synthesis is produced in India?... In spite of the antithesis between Communism and Fascism, there are certain traits in common. Both Communism and Fascism believe in the supremacy of the State over the individual. Both denounce parliamentary democracy. Both believe in party rule. Both believe in the dictatorship of the party and in the ruthless suppression of all dissenting minorities. Both believe in a planned industrial reorganisation of the country. These common traits will form the basis of the new synthesis.

The purpose of describing Bose and his thoughts is to demonstrate how the fever of nationalism had gripped India in the decades preceding Independence on 15 August 1947. Here was a man who was entranced by the most anti-Enlightenment ideologies, communism and fascism. Communism has killed over 100 million people all over the world; by the time he wrote so adoringly about his ideology, several million people had already perished in Stalin's Russia.

Unsurprisingly, Bose had little regard for the individual. Notice how insouciantly he talks about 'the supremacy of the State over the individual'; also how nonchalantly he discusses the need for the synthesis of the two modern evils. And yet he became the leader of the Congress Party. In fact, in 1939, he won the election for party president against Mahatma Gandhi's preferred candidate, Pattabhi Sitaramayya. Such was the sway that this mélange of Hitler, Stalin, and Mussolini had on the people of India.

Nobody has mentioned this before, but Gandhi's great contribution to India was not that he led the nation against the British but that he shielded us from the twentieth century. This was the century in which violent ideologies, both from the Left and the Right, brought untold miseries to mankind; millions died in wars and armed conflicts; many more perished in the endeavours for the creation of New Man and New Society. But Gandhi somehow managed to keep the violent passions and ferocious enthusiasms of the twentieth century at bay; his confused, medieval irrationalism triumphed over all manner of dangerous, modern irrationalism. His thinking may not have been mature or valuable, but his personal charisma and astute leadership did not allow the pathologies of the twentieth century to become full-blown cases. The meteoric rise and the subsequent marginalisation of Bose show that the ground was fertile for Nazi-like nationalism in India, but the danger was tackled primarily by Gandhi. Needless to say, Gandhi's pacifism infuriated Bose.

Nationalism thrived on the us-them chasm: 'we' were nationalist Indians with the solitary objective of political liberation; 'they' were the British, whose exit, we presumed, would bring deliverance. But we were wrong. As Tagore wrote in *Nationalism*:

> Those of us in India who have come under the delusion that mere political freedom will make us free have accepted their lessons from the West as the gospel truth and lost their faith in humanity. We must remember whatever weakness we cherish in our society will become the source of danger in politics. The same inertia which leads us to our idolatry of dead forms in social institutions will create in our politics, prison-houses with immovable walls.

With politics gaining ascendance, the reforming spirit evaporated; whatever association with the Enlightenment ideals that had survived the onslaught of nationalist mythology, almost completely disappeared after India gained Independence from the British on 15 August 1947. Reason took a back seat; everything that did not fit into the project of 'nation-building' was maligned and finally banished.

The Indian state grew in size, strength, scope, and severity. Therefore, freedom of expression and economic liberty were the first casualties. Consider the case of Nirad C. Chaudhari: his first book, *The Autobiography of an Unknown Indian* published in 1951, was hailed as a masterpiece. But it also had many remarks and observations which infuriated nationalists. What, however, brought trouble for Chaudhuri was the book's dedication:

> To the memory of the British Empire in India,
> Which conferred subject hood upon us,
> But withheld citizenship.
> To which yet every one of us threw out the challenge:
> 'Civis Britannicus sum'
> Because all that was good and living within us
> Was made, shaped and quickened
> By the same British rule.

Chaudhuri faced considerable persecution. He was forced to give up a government job, denied his pension, and blacklisted as a writer in India. It was perhaps the only case in the history of mankind that an author faced the wrath of the authorities because of the dedication of his book. As Chaudhuri's friend and author Khushwant Singh commented: 'The wogs took the bait and having read only dedication sent up howls of protest.'

Nationalism did not lose its virulence after Independence. Human autonomy, which according to Kant is 'the means and end of Enlightenment', fell victim to the First Amendment of the Constitution, which took place after just fifteen months of the Constitution coming into effect on 26 January 1950.

The Original Sin

This was the beginning of the curtailment of freedom of speech and expression as well as of property rights. The concept of 'reasonable restrictions' was brought in to curb the freedom of expression. The First Amendment proved to be the Original Sin, for the concept of reasonable restrictions is deeply flawed.

We were rendered, at best, partially free, for the 'reasonable restrictions' appended to the right to freedom of speech and expression in Article 19 (a) empowered the State to curb this fundamental right whenever it wished to. Restrictions can be imposed for the maintenance of 'the security of the State, friendly relations with foreign States, public order, decency or morality, or in relation to contempt of court, defamation or incitement to an offence.' Since the concepts of the security of the state, friendly relations with foreign States, and maintenance of public order or decency are comprehensive enough to restrict the freedom of expression in every conceivable manner, the sphere of freedom has shrunk considerably. For instance, the government cannot be accused of betraying the Constitution if it comes down heavily against an author who exposes the role of any country, including Pakistan, in fomenting violence in India. Technically, a ban on his writings would not be *mala fide*, if the government says that it wants to improve ties with Pakistan and his writings may jeopardise the ameliorating Indo-Pak relations. Similarly, decency and morality are vague and, therefore, can be applied arbitrarily.

Compare this with the First Amendment to the American Constitution which protects the freedom of expression. The First Amendment says, 'Congress [the US Parliament] shall make no law respecting an establishment of religion, or prohibiting the free exercise thereof; or abridging the freedom of speech, or of the press; or the right of the people peaceably to assemble, and to petition the Government for a redress of grievances.' Unsurprisingly, the US is called the land of the free, while India is becoming the land of the freaky and the tetchy.

So, it is not surprising that not a single day passes when some political party, social organisation, religious group, or downright publicity-hungry outfit does not demand a ban on some movie, book, exhibition, video remix, *etc*. The Hindus want to ban the nude painting of Saraswati (Hindu goddess of knowledge, wisdom, learning music, and arts) by M.F. Husain; the Muslims want anything even vaguely against Islam to be proscribed; a few Sikh groups campaigned against the film, *Jo Bole So Nihal*, even though it was cleared by their supreme body, the SGPC; many Christians were against the showing of the movie, *The Da Vinci Code*. Then there are governments and politicians that love moral-policing: Former Union Health Minister A. Ramadoss wanted to ban the depiction of smoking scenes in films and on TV. Liberty is assaulted every day. What is worse is that such assaults continue unabated; they do not cause revulsion among people at large; indeed, some assaults actually enjoy considerable public support.

The other objective of the First Amendment to the Constitution was to undermine the Fundamental Right of Property; the inexorable logic of the arguments posited by the Amendment ultimately led to the abolition this right from the list of fundamental rights; a 1978 Amendment downgraded it to a mere legal right. In India and many other countries, generations have been tutored into believing that the institution of property is evil, that it is an essential feature of capitalism which is based on 'profit-making' and which necessarily involves 'exploitation of man by man.' But, in reality, property is inextricably linked with human freedom. John Locke, the father of classical liberalism, wrote that 'every man has a property in his own person: this no body has any right to but himself. The labour of his body, and the work of his hands, we may say, are properly his.'

In terms of ontology, man is more than 'labour of his body, and the work of his hands,' and working of his mind: he is the embodiment of self-affirmation. The history of man is nothing but the story of his desire and endeavour to affirm his existence in the world. The entrepreneur who launches a business, the general who seeks glory, the soldier who volunteers for a dangerous mission, the revolutionary who endures torture, the politician who insists on a policy, the pontiff who preaches, the bureaucrat who brandishes the rulebook, the architect who takes up a challenging assignment, the engineer who decides to build a bridge against all odds, the painter who loses himself in the canvas, the sportsman who punishes his body to excel, the scientist who engrosses himself in abstractions—all these and other people do not strive merely for pecuniary gains and material comforts. Of course, physical well-being is extremely important, but there is also a desire to leave one's mark in the world; and for this, man strives to go beyond the necessary and the obvious, to go where no man has gone before. In the process, he reaches out of himself. Camus said man is the only creature who refuses to be what he is. This 'reaching-outness' is the being of man.

The attack on the institution of property is, therefore, an attack on the essential feature of man, an attack on his 'reaching-outness.' 'Since man has to sustain his life by his own effort, the man who has no right to the product of his effort has no means to sustain his life,' wrote Ayn Rand, adding that 'The man who produces while others dispose of his product, is a slave.' Actually, the denial of the concept of property is worse than that; it is much more than the individual versus state issue: the attack on property is actually the negation of the being of man. It deprives the individual of his humanity. Man is rendered a subhuman entity, incapable of surviving in the world. His lot is made worse than that of a slave, for if I enslave somebody and force him to dispose of his product, I may still regard him as human; it is only under coercion that I snatch what belongs to him. But from an ontological perspective, the doctrines which are against the institution of property belittle the human being. The resultant political ideologies just follow the inexorable logic of ontological dwarfing. All these ideologies are essentially collectivist; and all of them, in varying degrees, opposed to freedom. Friedrich A. Hayek wrote:

> What our generation has forgotten is that the system of private property is the most important guarantee of freedom, not only for those who own property, but scarcely less for those who do not. It is only because the control of the means of production is divided among many people acting independently that nobody has complete power over us, that we as individuals can decide what to do with ourselves. If all it be nominally that of 'society' as a whole of that of a dictator, whoever exercises this control has complete power over us.

Therefore, by curtailing the freedom of expression and the right to property, the First Amendment to the Indian Constitution was quite comprehensive in its assault on human liberty *per se*; the comprehensiveness and the intensity of the assault increased in subsequent Amendments. One would have hoped for some substantive resistance to, if not stalling of, the shrinking of liberty. The 1950s and the 1960s could boast of a number of sincere politicians—for whom politics was not bereft of certain ideals and values. There was also a large intellectual class, trained in the universities and familiar with Enlightenment ideals and values.

Unfortunately, most politicians could not garner the courage to check the depredations of nationalism and socialism. It was only a small set of politicians, mainly from the Swatantra Party, who championed the cause of individual liberty and free enterprise. Founded by a prominent national leader Chakravarti Rajagopalachari, in August 1959, it could boast of towering intellectuals like Minoo Masani and K.M. Munshi. The party's twenty-one principles, as enshrined in its manifesto, were generally in harmony with classical liberal lines.

At the hustings, the party began well, getting 6.8 per cent of the total votes and eighteen seats in the third Lok Sabha (1962-67). In four major states—Bihar, Rajasthan, Gujarat, and Orissa—it emerged as the main Opposition party. It was the single largest Opposition party in the mid-1960s in Parliament with 8.7 per cent of the total votes and forty-four seats in the Fourth Lok Sabha (1967-71).

But it could not survive the onslaught of aggressive socialism, which was the hallmark of Indira Gandhi's ascendance. At any rate, the limited and temporary success of the Swatantra Party was more due to the sterling personality of its leading lights and the association of princes rather than the popularity of the ideas it propagated among the people. It was the socialist rhetoric that was becoming popular and politically remunerative. Even capitalists supported the parties wedded to socialism rather than to the party which stood for free economy.

And it was the intellectual class which—instead of upholding the genuine Enlightenment ideals of individual liberty and limited government—disseminated socialist concepts among the people. It behaved just like the priestly class of yore. The priests in earlier times fabricated genealogies for whichever brigand became the king, linking him to gods or mythical heroes; they also wrote the religious and secular laws to suit the interests of the ruling class. Similarly, intellectuals manufactured economic and political theories to justify socialism as practiced by the essentially Nehruvian Establishment. It was not very difficult to blend nationalism with socialism, for both are collectivist ideologies. Eminent historian Bipan Chandra, for instance, created 'usable' narratives—usable, that is, for the Establishment.

While the political nation, assisted by intellectuals, tightened its grip over India, social reform was neglected. The great institutions founded by the pioneers in the nineteenth century became trusts run by the pillars of society, by social entrepreneurs and bureaucrats, by the men and women related to the Establishment. Since members of the Establishment are not in the habit of raising fundamental questions and challenging conventional wisdom, there was hardly any reformer after Independence with the zeal of a Swami Dayanand or the drive of a Vidyasagar.

A couple of unsavoury developments took place. First, the Indian state—which under Nehruvian socialism was arrogating to itself all economic powers—donned the mantle of the social reformer. Second, a new type of social reformer came into being: the one relying on state action. The trend became prominent from the 1960s, when the Left-leaning intellectual, disillusioned by the mainstream communist parties, took upon himself to change the system. While the nineteenth century pioneers were rooted in tradition and just wanted to remove the rot in society, the new reformer viewed tradition *per se* as rot; the latter did not find any redeeming feature in the tradition and culture of the country; he was an activist rather than a reformer. While the nineteenth century reformer sought state intervention when it was unavoidable, his twentieth century descendant in Independent India primarily relied on the state. This was despite the fact that his vehicle was a 'non-governmental organisation'!

This did not mean that activists lacked idealism, commitment, or the capacity to sacrifice material comforts, though it is also true that a number of NGOs were into racketeering. But the bigger problem was that ideology rather than idealism was the motivating factor for the new reformer. His paradigm was fundamentally different from that of the nineteenth century reformer. Wedded to the Marxist principle that political power in the hands of people can redeem the society, he was more interested in legislation and government finances for reform.

It would be interesting to study the mind of the activist. Merriam-Webster defines 'activism' as 'a doctrine or practice that emphasises direct vigorous action especially in support of or opposition to one side of a controversial issue.' A social reformer too, does the same. Raja Ram Mohan Roy was one such person who emphasised direct vigorous action in support of the anti-Suttee legislation.

Over a period of time, however, words assume a life of their own. The word 'activist' is one such term. Though indistinguishable with the reformer of yore, the activist today is quite different from the reformer. While both stand for change, their attitudes towards the change are poles apart. The reformer wants the change to be gradual and, as far as possible, volitional; he relies on persuasion. On the other hand, the activist wants radical, drastic change—ban diesel vehicles immediately, implement food security at once, and so on. He wants to impose the change; and he relies on confrontation rather than persuasion. The reformer listens to the other side, and tries to address their concerns; the activist bulldozes the opponents who anyway represent 'vested interests.' This also explains the activist's endeavour to use the coercive instrumentality of the state to further his agenda. In short, reformers and activists have emerged as specimens of different species over the years. At any rate, reformers are on the verge of extinction. Unsurprisingly, the activist also has a disdain for experts, who use the scientific method of studying and analysing empirical evidence. The expert uses facts to come up with the big picture; the activist already knows what the big picture is and, thus, picks up facts selectively and fits them into it.

The new paradigm engendered two developments. First, the reformer, convinced of the class struggle and critical legal theories, focused on the fault-lines in society: he took up the cause of landless labourers, tribals, slum-dwellers, *etc.* Instead of helping the poor by enabling them to get out of the culture of poverty—*e.g*, by building educational institutions, as Christian missionaries and the Arya Samaj do—the new reformer instigated the poor to demand more and more freebies from the state. He was and is interested in the quantifiable—more budgetary allocation for education, more outlays for the social sector, new schemes for landless labourers and for tribals, better 'delivery mechanism,' *etc.* And he had little inclination for the unquantifiable and intangibles like changing the attitudes of the poor, improving their habits pertaining to education, thrift, women, *etc*; nor was he interested in instilling the virtues of responsibility and self-esteem in them.

The new paradigm prompted another development—a heightened awareness about and greater demands for entitlements in all sections of the society and not just among the poor. All of us—farmers, tribals, slum-dwellers, students, teachers, journalists, even businessmen—strive for goodies and/or succour from the government. Even investors in the stock market want the government 'to do something' when there is a crash. In general, for any problem, we say: 'The government should do something about it.' Unsurprisingly, government is gaining in size and strength, the individual is getting dwarfed, and India's jihad against Enlightenment ideals is intensifying every moment. It is in this context that we have to ponder over one question: is an Indian citizen today freer than he or she was on 14 August 1947? Freedom has two parts—expression and action.

We have seen how the First Amendment shackled both the freedom of expression and that of action. The British would bristle at books, articles, poems, *etc.*, that they found seditious; beyond that, they did not have much of a problem with writers, poets, and other creative persons. In cinema, for instance, there were passionate lip kiss scenes; they were bannedonly after Independence. As we mentioned earlier, artists and filmmakers have faced a number of problems for reasons other than political. If we have a dispassionate, non-nationalistic view, we will find that the sphere of the freedom of expression has shrunk after

Independence. Tagore was right: '... political freedom does not give us freedom when our mind is not free.' Nor does political freedom mean anything if there is little freedom of action. Since Independence, the state has continued to encroach upon the rights of people, be it the captains of industry, the struggling entrepreneurs, small traders, street vendors, or the dance bar girls of Bombay.

What became free on 15 August 1947 was the Indian nation, not the people of India. In comparison, British rule was much better than what we have witnessed since that fateful day.

Chapter 1

Freedom of expression = Right to offend, right to blaspheme

I disagree with what you say, but I will defend to the death your right to say it—Voltaire

I begin with the pertinent question: is it possible to have freedom of expression which is not absolute? The answer is a big 'no'. Freedom of expression ought to be absolute, or it is not freedom at all.

The immediate objection to this assertion, especially in the Indian context, is that there is no point in offending people. Novels, short stories, and poetry can be and are being written, and movies made, without hurting the sentiments of groups and communities, the objectors say. After all, they point out, a huge amount of literature is created and a large number of films produced, without objections from people. Why then are writers and filmmakers coming up with works that hold the potential to offend?

John Stuart Mill, arguably the greatest champion of 'the fullest liberty of professing and discussing,' talked about what came to be known as the Harm Principle: '... the only purpose for which power can be rightfully exercised over any member of a civilised community, against his will, is to prevent harm to others.' An insidious development is the introduction of the so-called Offence Principle. American philosopher Joel Feinberg in 1985 recommended an Offence Principle to act as a guide to public censure. According to him, Mill's Harm Principle is not sufficient to check wrongful behaviour:

> ...it is always a good reason in support of a proposed criminal prohibition that it would probably be an effective way of preventing serious offense... to persons other than the actor, and that it is probably a necessary means to that end... *The principle asserts, in effect, that the prevention of offensive conduct is properly the state's business.* (emphasis added).

Feinberg favoured the legal prohibition of some forms of expression if they were very offensive, though he recommended lower penalties for offence than for harm. Feinberg suggests that a number of factors need to be taken into account when applying the Offence Principle including the extent, duration, and social value of the speech, the ease with which it can be avoided, the motives of the speaker, the number of people offended, the intensity of the offense, and the general interest of the community at large. The Offence Principle intends to legitimately prohibit some forms of expression because they are very offensive. He, however, agrees that offending someone is less serious than harming someone.

In the Stanford Encyclopedia of Philosophy, Professor David Van Mill of the University of Western Australia wrote:

> One of the most impressive arguments for this position comes from Joel Feinberg, who suggests that the Harm Principle cannot shoulder all of the work necessary for a principle of free speech. In some instances, Feinberg suggests, we also need an Offense Principle that can act as a guide to public censure. The basic idea is that the Harm Principle sets the bar too high and that we can legitimately prohibit some forms of expression because they are very offensive. Offending someone is less serious than harming someone, so the penalties imposed should be less severe than those for causing harm. As Feinberg notes, however, this has not always been the case and he cites a number of instances in the US where penalties for sodomy and consensual incest have ranged from twenty years imprisonment to the death penalty.

> These are victimless crimes and hence the punishment has to have a basis in the supposed offensiveness of the behavior rather than the harm that is caused.

Well, if there are laws and penalties that are too harsh, especially in victimless crimes, the cure is a healthy debate and possible revision, and certainly not their extension to free speech. As we shall see later, the formal acceptance of the Offence Principle—which in India has been practically accepted by the political class, public intellectuals, and the judiciary to some extent—will spell the death of freedom in liberal democracies.

Secondly, if 'prevention of offensive behaviour' becomes the state's business, as Feinberg wants it to become, politicians, bureaucrats, and judges would be further empowered at the expense of not only creative persons like writers and filmmakers but also common people. Further, the 'criminal prohibition' to prevent 'serious offense... to persons other than the actor' presupposes the role of a nanny on the part of the state. Needless to say, the presupposition is not only erroneous but also fraught with the dangers of paternal state.

The Harm Principle

The impression that we sometimes get is that Mill favoured some governmental control over the freedom of expression. It arises from confusing 'action' with 'expression of views.' The full passage is:

> The object of this Essay is to assert one very simple principle, as entitled to govern absolutely the dealings of society with the individual in the way of compulsion and control, whether the means used be physical force in the form of legal penalties, or the moral coercion of public opinion. That principle is that the sole end for which mankind are warranted, individually or collectively, in interfering with the *liberty of action* of any of their number, is self-protection. That the only purpose for which power can be rightfully exercised over any member of a civilised community, against his will, is to prevent harm to others. (emphasis added). [Introductory, *On Liberty*, John Stuart Mill]

It is unfortunate that even those who claim to champion the cause of liberty sometimes refuse to distinguish between the two. Consider prominent economist, classicist, and Niti Aayog member, Bibek Debroy whose article titled 'Politics of bans and rights' in *The Indian Express* on 28 November 2007, where he wrote:

> ...is an individual right ever absolute? It can't be, for it is conceivable that the exercise of my individual right might constrain yours, and there is a difference between exercising an individual right in my private domain and doing it in public. For instance, it might be fine for me to walk around nude in my apartment, but should I be allowed to do it in public? If I am a serial killer, exercise of my individual right might require me to murder people. Should that be allowed? Even in relatively free countries, including the US, freedom of expression is a relative not absolute right—defamation, obscenity, perjury, copyright violations, actions that incite hate, sedition and blasphemy are all instances where freedom of expression has been curbed in developed countries.

Notice how Debroy bypasses the Harm Principle. Also notice how he mixes various concepts—freedom of expression with freedom of action, defamation with perjury and copyright violations. Freedom of expression has little to do with perjury and copyright violations for these are crimes by their very definition and have little to do with freedom of expression: perjury is lying under oath, whereas copyright violations are about stealing somebody's intellectual property. Defamation, on the other hand, is related to freedom of expression—we shall come to this later. More misleading is the blurring of distinction between opinion and action. Loitering nude on streets and killing people are actions; airing of views, however controversial, unconventional, seditious, or blasphemous, is just a way of telling others what one thinks and feels about something. Mill is clear about the distinction. He wrote:

> No one pretends that actions should be as free as opinions. On the contrary, even opinions lose their immunity, when the circumstances in which they are expressed are such as to constitute their expression a positive instigation to some

> mischievous act. An opinion that corn-dealers are starvers of the poor, or that private property is robbery, ought to be unmolested when simply circulated through the press, but may justly incur punishment when delivered orally to an excited mob assembled before the house of a corn-dealer, or when handed about among the same mob in the form of a placard. Acts, of whatever kind, which, without justifiable cause, do harm to others, may be, and in the more important cases absolutely require to be, controlled by the unfavorable sentiments, and, when needful, by the active interference of mankind. The liberty of the individual must be thus far limited; he must not make himself a nuisance to other people.

Opinions ought to be freer than actions because words break no bones. Mill would not accept any curbs on the freedom of speech except in rare circumstances—to 'an excited mob' against corn-dealers 'before the house of a corn-dealer'; that is, when the harm to life, limb, and property of the targeted person is imminent. But then, in such situations, haranguing an angry mob is incitement to violence rather than an expression of opinion, and there is nothing improper in penalising incitement to violence. At any rate, such penalising would be against felonious intent and action rather than freedom of expression. When a mafia don orders his henchmen to eliminate a rival, he is not exercising his right to freedom of expression but triggering a crime. There is a difference between freedom of expression and incitement of crime.

A socialist is not only entitled to his view that private property is theft but also free to express it. He, however, crosses the line only when he convinces, coaxes, or instigates his followers to such an extent that they immediately carry out violent activities against propertied persons or property.

The indoctrination doctrine

It can be and is argued that incitement may not always be imminent or immediate. It is possible to fill the hearts and minds of a group with hatred against person(s), institution, religion or country on a long-term basis. Should indoctrination be allowed? As it is, Islamic terror and Maoist menace, to name the two biggest threats India faces, are problems for the people and the government. If freedom of expression is made absolute, it would be possible for the most venomous jihadists and hardcore Maoists to impart their violent doctrines. Would not that be a recipe for disaster? It may appear that unrestrained freedom of expression would give a fillip to, among other things, jihadist as well as Red terror, but a proper analysis would show otherwise.

To begin with, it must be made clear that these two problems have not been caused because of the freedom of expression as it exists in the country, nor would they be exacerbated if this freedom is made unlimited. They have been caused and exacerbated by politicians' machinations, their bad policies, and their reluctance to uphold the rule of law. The rule of law, it may be mentioned, is the necessary condition for freedom of expression in an open society.

Maoism came into being in the late 1960s. It has seen several crests and troughs. A variety of factors were responsible for its birth and current virulence—socialist economic policies, bad governance, and the lack of political will to combat Leftwing violence. Even today, the Maoist sympathisers openly propagate the justness of the Maoist cause. So, absolute freedom of expression will not aggravate the problem.

As for jihadist violence, it needs to be emphasised that the curtailment of freedom of expression has actually boosted the morale of Islamic fundamentalists, emboldening them to directly and indirectly help terrorists. A watershed in the history of freedom of expression in India was the ban of Salman Rushdie's *Satanic Verses* in 1988; it proved that the Indian political class could be subdued by a mix of rhetoric, threat, and downright violence. Published on 26 September 1988 in the UK, it was reviewed by the prominent journalist and author Khushwant Singh in the *Illustrated Weekly of India*. He recommended a ban on the book arguing that it could lead to trouble. Another journalist-author who called for proscription was M.J. Akbar, now a junior minister in the government led by the supposedly Rightwing Bharatiya Janata Party. Parliamentarian and editor of the monthly magazine *Muslim India*, Syed Shahabuddin, petitioned the Rajiv Gandhi government on the same lines. The government immediately responded and banned the book on 5 October. Years later, Bangladeshi author Taslima Nasreen was also hunted and persecuted by Muslim fanatics, and she too received minimal support from India.

An intended consequence of proscription and persecution has been the demise of all meaningful debate on Islam; everybody knows that any critical observation about the theology and practice of Islam would attract opprobrium and possibly prosecution. All writers and journalists know that criticism would make them vulnerable to the accusation of being bigoted and fascist. If such criticism comes from a Muslim, his predicament could be worse; even his physical existence would be in danger. There have been cases where fundamentalist Muslim politicians have tried to incite violence against those who were critical of Islam. As a result, we now have a perverse inversion of the freedom of expression: while writers and artists are restrained from freely expressing themselves, those who are opposed to this freedom are rarely restrained. The perversity is comprehensive. The *views* the illiberal elements find unpalatable are suppressed but the *violence* they engender is tolerated.

The unintended consequence of this is the malaise that has spread among other sections of Indian society. The success of retrograde elements in Muslim society has encouraged similar elements in other communities to impose their narrow viewpoints. Thus we had the medievalist Hindus violently protesting against some of the paintings of the late M.F. Husain on the grounds that these hurt their sentiments. Another painter, Jatin Das, also had to face the ire of Hindu zealots.

Roots of fear

Where does this fear of absolute freedom of expression come from?

The fear has its roots in the belief that there is a reality (or Reality) which can be misrepresented or distorted if the freedom of expression is absolute. This presupposes a universally accepted definition of the reality. But the fact is that no such definition exists; there are as many definitions of reality as there are philosophers and philosophies. There are Christian theologians interpreting the faith in numerous ways; there are six orthodox Hindu schools of philosophy, with several sub-schools; there are Marxists again following countless lines; there are Western conservatives (all of them ardently anti-state, Burkeans in harmony with tradition); there are libertarians (followers of Ayn Rand and others); there are postmodern thinkers who actually do not believe in any reality. It is a long list. What then is the reality or ultimate reality? What is the truth or the Truth?

I do not claim that reality does not exist, or as Kant said, that it is unknowable (*noumenon*); this question is not pertinent to my thesis. My assertion is that since there is no universally accepted understanding of (ultimate) reality, the question of its misrepresentation or distortion does not arise.

Let us come down from the metaphysical plane and concentrate on the mundane aspects of life. Let us discuss topics like the state, market, society, individual rights, and property. Again, we face the same plurality of views. What is the state? Marxists define the term in a way with which libertarians and conservatives can never agree with. What should be the role of the state? While Left-leaning thinkers would argue for its big role in the economy, libertarians and conservatives would like it to keep away from the market. Should the market take care of itself or should it be kept under the watchful eye of government functionaries and regulators? Again, there is a wide divergence of views. For instance, Ayn Rand is against regulators, whereas in India even those who are considered pro-market favour regulators.

What is society? Is it organic and more than the sum-total of individuals as Burke and many conservatives believe? Is society, as Burke put it, 'a partnership not only between those who are living, but between those who are living, those who are dead, and those who are to be born?'His contemporary and antagonist Thomas Paine (1737–1809) couldn't disagree more. In *Rights of Man*, he wrote, 'Every age and generation must be as free to act for itself in all cases as the age and generations which preceded it... Every generation is, and must be, competent to all the purposes which its occasions require. It is the living, and not the dead, that are to be accommodated.' In more recent times, Rand disagreed with the Burkean definition of society; in her scheme of things, everything is subservient to the individual and his rights. Interestingly, both Burke and Rand are placed on the right of the ideological spectrum.

Individual rights are also understood in vastly different ways by thinkers of different persuasions. Those on the Right want nothing but freedom from the clutches of government, freedom to be left alone—*laissez faire*. The Leftists, on the other hand, find such freedom vacuous; they talk about the rights to food, work, education, *etc.*, all of which requires a big, strong, and generous state. For conservatives and libertarians, economic freedom means the liberty to doing business without government interference so long as no laws are broken; for socialists, economic freedom means the opposite.

Similarly, on property there are diametrically opposite views across the ideological spectrum. While the Left views it as the result of exploitation (if not downright theft), the Right regards it as the cornerstone of liberty.

Therefore, there is no unanimity on any kind of reality, metaphysical or mundane. I will reiterate that this is not a thesis promoting epistemological nihilism; on the contrary, mine is an attempt to undermine such nihilism. This nihilism is actually promoted by the postmodern dogma in association with various anti-Enlightenment tendencies like political correctness, multiculturalism, and Islamism.

The only way we can know any truth is by allowing the free play of ideas in the arena of public discourse, a veritable *laissez faire*in the marketplace of ideas. A genuine quest for knowledge and a yearning for wisdom (or philosophy, which is etymologically, 'love for wisdom') is an onward march to gain more facts; we shall realise as many truths as possible. The quest may or may not lead us to the 'Ultimate Reality' (if it exists), but we can hope to become wiser. However, this march is impossible without unrestrained freedom of expression.

If there is no consensus even among the greatest philosophers about the nature of any kind of reality, it is the apogee of hubris, and of dirigisme, to assume that politicians, bureaucrats, and judges know what the reality is and what is its distortion. And if these personages don't know what the reality is, they cannot deliver any verdict on what its distortion is.

Controversy is inevitable

A large number of truths came to be acknowledged as such without much fuss, but there are many which were preceded by long and often acrimonious debates and sometimes also with violence. Acrimony takes place because somebody or some group feels offended by a truth. It is often argued that we must avoid the truths which violate the Offence Principle, for the consequences could be apocalyptic.

The Galileo affair needs special mention in the context of the Offence Principle. Galileo published his *Sidereus Nuncius* (Starry Messenger) in 1610. This was based on the observations that he had made with his telescope. Some of these discoveries—lunar mountains, small moons around Jupiter, the phases of Venus and sunspots—indirectly undermined geocentric Christian cosmology. They harmed nobody but offended the sensibilities of people in an age in which religious faith was a great, if not the ultimate, concern. Had Galileo decided *not* to offend the Christians—and this would have been a rewarding option—he would have deprived the world of important truths and science would have been poorer. He was not granted freedom of expression; he had to grab it. And he did offend many—and suffered because of the 'offence.' Without the freedom to offend, as Salman Rushdie said, freedom of expression ceases to exist.

There are many other instances where science offers explanations which conflict with religious beliefs, but the science-religion conflict is beyond the scope of our thesis. What is pertinent here is that even religions that have evolved over the centuries could not have done so without challenging the established orthodoxies and offending many people: Jesus Christ propagated beliefs which offended many people, leading to his crucifixion; Shankaracharya (788-821) famously disputed with great theologians; Martin Luther enraged the then Pope's clergy. In fact, it is in religion rather than in science that new expositions are generally frowned upon.

An erroneous postulate

To say that freedom of expression should be curtailed lest it offend or hurt the sentiments of people, or some people, implicitly accepts a ludicrous postulate: that all facts and truths that mankind ought to know are known and that any new expositions would merely distort truths. One need not be a philosopher to say that the postulate is not only ludicrous but also smacks of hubris and complacency.

At any rate, the Offence Principle would end up banishing philosophy and any serious contemplation. As Bertrand Russell wrote in *The Problems of Philosophy*:

> Philosophy is to be studied, not for the sake of any definite answers to its questions since no definite answers can, as a rule, be known to be true, but rather for the sake of the questions themselves; because these questions enlarge our conception of what is possible, enrich our intellectual imagination and diminish the dogmatic assurance which closes the mind against speculation; but above all because, through the greatness of the universe which philosophy contemplates, the mind also is rendered great, and becomes capable of that union with the universe which constitutes its highest good.

Chapter 2

Freedom of expression in independent India

When India became independent on 15 August1947, many thought that this would gradually, if not automatically result in greater individual freedom. After all, the British imperialists had quit; soon the vestiges of repression would also go. The land of Tagore's dream seemed within sight: 'Where the mind is without fear and the head is held high... Where the clear stream of reason has not lost its way/Into the dreary desert sand of dead habit...'

But, alas, that was not to be! Imperialism was gone, but an equally, if not more constraining, tendency replaced it—nationalism. Nationalism did not lose its virulent sting after Independence. Human autonomy, which was the defining feature of the Enlightenment, fell victim to the First Amendment of the Constitution, which took place just fifteen months after the Constitution came into effect on 26 January 1950. The website of the Ministry of Law and Justice lists the Statement of Objects and Reasons appended to the Constitution (First Amendment) Bill 1951 which was enacted as the Constitution (First Amendment) Act 1951:

> During the last fifteen months of the working of the Constitution, certain difficulties have been brought to light by

> judicial decisions and pronouncements specially in regard to the chapter on fundamental rights. The citizen's right to freedom of speech and expression guaranteed by article 19(1)(a) has been held by some courts to be so comprehensive as not to render a person culpable even if he advocates murder and other crimes of violence. In other countries with written constitutions, freedom of speech and of the press is not regarded as debarring the State from punishing or preventing abuse of this freedom. The citizen's right to practise any profession or to carry on any occupation, trade or business conferred by article 19(1)(g) is subject to reasonable restrictions which the laws of the State may impose 'in the interests of general public.' While the words cited are comprehensive enough to cover any scheme of nationalisation which the State may undertake, it is desirable to place the matter beyond doubt by a clarificatory addition to article 19(6). Another article in regard to which unanticipated difficulties have arisen is article 31. The validity of agrarian reform measures passed by the State Legislatures in the last three years has, in spite of the provisions of clauses (4) and (6) of article 31, formed the subject-matter of dilatory litigation, as a result of which the implementation of these important measures, affecting large numbers of people, has been held up.
>
> The main objects of this Bill are, accordingly to amend article 19 for the purposes indicated above and to insert provisions fully securing the constitutional validity of zamindari abolition laws in general and certain specified State Acts in particular. The opportunity has been taken to propose a few minor amendments to other articles in order to remove difficulties that may arise.

This was the beginning of the curtailment of freedom of speech and expression and property rights. The concept of 'reasonable restrictions' was brought in to curb the freedom of expression. The First Amendment proved to be the Original Sin, for the concept of reasonable restrictions is deeply flawed.

Partially free people

We were rendered, at best, partially free, for the 'reasonable restrictions' appended to the Right to Freedom of Speech and Expression in Article 19(a) empowered the State to curb this fundamental right whenever it wished to. Restrictions can be imposed for the maintenance of 'the security of the State, friendly relations with foreign States, public order, decency or morality, or in relation to contempt of court, defamation or incitement to an offence.' Since the concepts of the security of the state, friendly relations with foreign states and maintenance of public order or decency are comprehensive enough to restrict the freedom of expression in every conceivable manner, the sphere of freedom has shrunk considerably. For instance, the government cannot be accused of betraying the Constitution if it comes down heavily against an author who exposes the role of any country, including Pakistan, in fomenting violence in India. Technically, a ban on his writings would not be *mala fide*, if the government says that it wants to improve ties with Pakistan and his writings may jeopardise the improving Indo-Pak relations. Similarly, decency and morality are vague and therefore, can be applied arbitrarily.

It needs to be mentioned that the curtailment of Article 19 was not the result of some tyrant scheming to intellectually subdue the people. While the ruler at that time, Jawaharlal Nehru, Independent India's first Prime Minister, was illiberal, he was not a scheming dictator. It was the desire of the nation, along with the ill-conceived notion of Nehru and his coterie, that the freedom of expression be restricted. Never at ease with the main Enlightenment ideal of individual liberty, the Indian nation manufactured chains to shackle the citizen. This was the reason that there was hardly any resistance to the curbing of the freedom of expression. This was, and is, a danger greater than the wickedness of a dictator. The people, as citizens and as constituents of the nation, had fallen in love with the chains that bound them.

Chapter 3

First Amendment: American and Indian

As a Republic, we began well with regard to liberty. When the Constitution came into force on 26 January 1950, it was arguably the most liberal one in the world, even more than that of the American one. As our Supreme Court noted in its judgment abrogating the odious Section 66A of the Information Technology Act: 'whereas the US First Amendment speaks of freedom of speech and of the press, without any reference to "expression", Article 19(1)(a) speaks of freedom of speech and expression without any reference to "the press".' In short, the Founding Fathers of our Republic envisaged liberty in its fullest form—not only of journalists and public speakers, but also of poets, littérateurs and filmmakers, among others.

It needs to be mentioned that in the United States, speech and press are explicitly, as well as unambiguously protected; other forms of expression are not. This was done by the First Amendment to the American Constitution:

> Congress [the US Parliament] shall make no law respecting an establishment of religion, or prohibiting the free exercise thereof; or abridging the freedom of speech, or of the press; or the right of the people peaceably to assemble, and to petition the Government for a redress of grievances.

The First Amendment (1951) in India, on the other hand, was introduced to undermine the freedom of expression. Our Constitution provides [Article 19(1)(a)] the right to 'freedom of speech and expression.' The First Amendment paved the path for eroding this right. As we mentioned in the first chapter, it offered a most specious ground for curtailing this right. According to the official version, 'The citizen's right to freedom of speech and expression guaranteed by Article 19(1)(a) has been held by some courts to be so comprehensive as not to render a person culpable even if he advocates murder and other crimes of violence.'

As we argued earlier, there is a clear distinction between words and actions; a tendency to confuse the two leads to the erosion of liberty. If some judges were unable to differentiate between the freedom of expression and the advocacy of murder and violent crimes, the remedy lay in educating, reprimanding, or removing them, and certainly not in delivering a deadly blow to a pillar of democracy. Unfortunately, Parliament at that time found it fit to impose 'reasonable restrictions' on the freedom of expression.

This is not to say that the freedom of expression is unfettered all over the world. Even in the US, there are restrictions on the freedom of speech. These exceptions also enjoy the approval of the United States Supreme Court. These restrictions have evolved over time. They pertain to cases involving incitement, false statements of fact, obscenity, child pornography, military personnel, prisoners, *etc.*

Imminent lawless action

The fundamental difference between the two countries with regard to the freedom of expression is that while exceptions to the constitutional right of free speech have to be made in the US, the restrictions are constitutionally imposed in India. In matters related to incitement, the US Supreme Court has held, in Brandenburg v. Ohio (1969), that 'advocacy of the use of force' is unprotected when it is 'directed to inciting or producing imminent lawless action' and is 'likely to incite or produce such action.'

The appellant, Clarence Brandenburg, a leader of a Ku Klux Klan group, was convicted under the Ohio Criminal Syndicalism statute for 'advocat[ing]... the duty, necessity, or propriety of crime, sabotage, violence, or unlawful methods of terrorism as a means of accomplishing industrial or political reform' and for voluntarily assembling with any society, group, or assemblage of persons formed to teach or advocate the doctrines of criminal syndicalism. 'He was fined $1,000 and sentenced to one to ten years' imprisonment,' according to the website of the Cornell Law University School[1]:

> The appellant challenged the constitutionality of the criminal syndicalism statute under the First and Fourteenth Amendments to the United States Constitution, but the intermediate appellate court of Ohio affirmed his conviction without opinion... [The Supreme Court of Ohio dismissed his appeal for the reason that no substantial constitutional question exists herein.'

The appellant telephoned an announcer-reporter on the staff of a Cincinnati television station and invited him to come to a Ku Klux Klan 'rally' to be held at a farm in Hamilton County. With the cooperation of the organisers, the reporter and a cameraman attended the meeting and filmed the events. Portions of the films were later broadcast on the local station and on a national network. The website quoting the Brandenburg v. Ohio (1969) verdict said:

> The prosecution's case rested on the films and on testimony identifying the appellant as the person who communicated with the reporter and who spoke at the rally. The State also introduced into evidence several articles appearing in the film, including a pistol, a rifle, a shotgun, ammunition, a Bible, and a red hood worn by the speaker in the films.

One film showed twelve hooded figures, some of whom carried firearms. They were gathered around a large wooden cross, which they burned. No one was present other than the participants and the newsmen who made the film. Most of the words uttered during the scene were incomprehensible when the film was projected, but scattered phrases could be understood that were derogatory of Negroes and, in one instance, of Jews. Another scene on the same film showed Brandenburg, in Klan regalia, making a speech:

1 See https://www.law.cornell.edu/supremecourt/text/395/444

> This is an organisers' meeting. We have had quite a few members here today which are—we have hundreds, hundreds of members throughout the State of Ohio. I can quote from a newspaper clipping from the Columbus, Ohio, Dispatch, five weeks ago Sunday morning. The Klan has more members in the State of Ohio than does any other organisation. We're not a revengent organisation, but if our President, our Congress, our Supreme Court, continues to suppress the white, Caucasian race, it's possible that there might have to be some revengeance taken.
>
> We are marching on Congress July the Fourth, four hundred thousand strong. From there, we are dividing into two groups, one group to march on St. Augustine, Florida, the other group to march into Mississippi. Thank you.

The second film showed six hooded figures one of whom, later identified as the Brandenburg, repeated a speech very similar to that recorded on the first film. The reference to the possibility of 'revengeance' was omitted, and one sentence was added: 'Personally, I believe the nigger should be returned to Africa, the Jew returned to Israel.' Though some of the figures in the films carried weapons, the speaker did not.

The Ohio Criminal Syndicalism Statute, enacted in 1919, was invoked to prosecute Brandenburg. From 1917 to 1920, identical or quite similar laws were adopted by twenty States and two territories. In 1927, the US Supreme Court sustained the constitutionality of such legal provisions in Whitney v. California (1927). Then the US Supreme Court ruled in Brandenburg v. Ohio (1969):

> The Court upheld the statute on the ground that, without more, 'advocating' violent means to effect political and economic change involves such danger to the security of the State that the State may outlaw it. But Whitney has been thoroughly discredited by later decisions. These later decisions have fashioned the principle that the constitutional guarantees of free speech and free press do not permit a State to forbid or proscribe advocacy of the use of force or of law violation except where such advocacy is directed to *inciting or producing imminent lawless action* and is likely to incite or produce such action.(emphasis added)

The court pointed out that 'the mere abstract teaching... of the moral propriety or even moral necessity for a resort to force and violence is not the same as preparing a group for violent action and steeling it to such action.' A statute which fails to draw this distinction impermissibly intrudes upon the freedoms guaranteed by the First and Fourteenth Amendments to the US Constitution. It sweeps within its condemnation speech which US Constitution has immunised from governmental control, the court pointed out. Measured by this test, Ohio's Criminal Syndicalism Act cannot be sustained, it added.

The 'imminent lawless action' test, however, was the culmination of evolution, the fruition of extensive debates in which the most ardent champions of liberty and the brightest jurists participated. In 1917, the legendary American jurist Oliver Wendell Holmes pronounced the 'clear and present danger' criterion which could be used to abridge free speech:

> The most stringent protection of free speech would not protect a man falsely shouting 'fire!'in a theater and causing a panic... The question in every case is whether the words used are used in such circumstances and are of such a nature as to create a clear and present danger that they will bring about the substantive evils that Congress has a right to prevent.

Two important points need to be made here:first, Holmes does not say that any deliberate statement should attract a penalty. If a man plays a prank in, say, a gathering of friends about fire without it leading to harm, he still enjoys the protection of free speech; second, if there *is* a fire and his scream causes a stampede and a few casualties, he is still protected, even if the fire were minor.

Sphere of liberty

Before the 'clear and present danger test', actions exhibiting a 'bad tendency' were punishable. Evidently, anything could be construed or misconstrued as pertaining to a bad tendency, thus augmenting the scope of state interventions—which in this context would be nothing but repression resulting in a curtailment of liberties. When government officials and prosecutors are forced to prove that a clear and present danger does exist, they have to be more specific. The 'imminent lawless action test' made their job even more difficult.

Over the years, the highest court in the US has expanded the sphere of liberty, thus concomitantly shrinking that of the state in its rulings. In India, on the other hand, it is the sphere of liberty that has shrunk because of the actions of various players such as the central and state governments, political parties and leaders, their front organisations, tetchy groups, wannabe celebrities, publicity seekers, and downright blackmailers.

Chapter 4

The Left and the Right of freedom

Our opinion makers malign Rightists as being illiberal, intolerant, and retrograde. Therefore, Bharatiya Janata Party leader and India's foremost conservative Subramanian Swamy's challenge to hate speech laws in the Supreme Court may appear odd—an exception to the rule that conservatives are against the freedom of expression. But, as it often happens, the truth is exactly the opposite of what the popes and archbishops of public discourse say it is.

Swamy has said that several provisions of the Indian Penal Code dealing with offences of 'hate speech' violate the fundamental right to freedom of expression as enshrined in the Constitution. He has mentioned Sections 153, 153A,153B, 295, 295A, 298, and 505 in this context. He has rightly asserted that these legal provisions are used to penalise the citizens of India in the exercise of their right to freedom of expression, and should therefore be invalidated.

If accepted by the apex court, this invalidation would be one of the biggest victories for liberty in India in the last one hundred years, to be ranked alongside Justice H.R. Khanna's note of dissent in 1976 that upheld fundamental rights against the deluge of Indira Gandhi's tyranny. Referring to the restrictive sections, Swamy said in his petition:

> All these sections do not have any safeguards within which a person can publicise his analysis of various nuanced truths of interaction between groups which differ on the basis of religion, race, place of birth, residence, language, caste or community.

The governments in Independent India should have provided the necessary safeguards to uphold the cause of liberty, but they did the exact opposite. Right from the beginning, our political masters tried to shrink rather than expand the sphere of liberty. The very First Amendment to the Constitution, as we noticed, introduced 'reasonable restrictions' on freedom of expression. The purpose was to ban or subdue any opinion, whether on the Left or the Right, that was unfavourable to Jawaharlal Nehru, the self-righteous politician whom intellectuals regard as a great liberal.

The instant provocations for the First Amendment were: ban on Romesh Thapar's Left-leaning magazine *Crossroads* by the Madras government which was set aside by courts on the grounds that it was *ultra vires* of the Constitutional provisions related to the freedom of expression; and Nehru's displeasure with the RSS mouthpiece, *Organiser*.

Therefore the Nehru government decided to undermine the freedom of expression and other fundamental rights, thus initiating a process which ultimately led to the scrapping of one fundamental right, the right to property, in 1978 and weakening of all fundamental rights in general.

We are fed the narrative that Nehru was an erudite liberal who had the temperament and tenderness of a poet, and the prudence of a statesman. Few would doubt his erudition, but fewer would call him tolerant if all the facts about the First Amendment and his other misdemeanours are made public—which are not because of the conspiracy of silence by Leftists and liberals, and the ignorance of Indian Rightists. In its 28 May1951 issue, the *Time* magazine gave a vivid description of Nehru's intolerance:

> Part of the Indian press, said [Nehru], is dirty, indulges in 'vulgarity, indecency and falsehood.' To teach it manners, Nehru proposed an amendment to India's constitution that would impose severe restrictions on freedom of speech and expression. He asked for power to curb the press and to punish persons and newspapers for 'contempt of court, defamation and incitement to an offense.' Nehru told Parliament: 'It has become a matter of the

> deepest distress to me to see the way in which the less responsible news sheets are being conducted… not injuring me or this House much, but poisoning the minds of the younger generation.'

Nehru's illiberality evoked considerable response in Parliament, the fiercest from Syama Prasad Mookerjee, who was earlier Minister of Industry in the Nehru Cabinet and who went on to found the Bharatiya Jana Sangh, which would later evolve into the BJP. Mukherjee fought the First Amendment tooth and nail. According to the *Time* report:

Mookerjee (to Nehru): You've got 240 supporters in this House, but outside in the country millions are against you.

Nehru (shaking his fists): [Your] statements are scandalous...

Mookerjee: Your intolerance is scandalous…

Nehru (shouting): Any person who says that this amendment of mine curbs the liberty of the press utters lies…

As Nehru explained it: 'We should not only give the press freedom, but make it understand that freedom.'

Notice the self-righteousness of Nehru: he did not realise that freedom is an inalienable right of human beings which can be given only by God, if you are a believer, or by nature, if you are not. At any rate, no government gives freedom as a gift to the people, certainly not the government run by a man as illiberal as Nehru. Freedom is the defining feature of man, his inalienable right, not an entitlement which can be withdrawn at will.

Nehru justified the First Amendment citing something as nebulous as the 'interests of the general public.' He said:

> During the last fifteen months of the working of the Constitution, certain difficulties have been brought to light by judicial decisions and pronouncements especially with regard to the chapter on fundamental rights. The citizen's right to freedom of speech and expression guaranteed by Article 19(1)(a) has been held by some courts to be so comprehensive as not to render a person culpable even if he advocates murder and other crimes of violence.

This was pure hogwash as no reading of Article 19(1)(a) can show that it can be used to incite a crime. It is important to note here that Nehru just wanted 'restrictions' on the freedom of expression; it was the Select Committee that insisted on the adjective 'reasonable'. And yet we are told that Nehru was a great liberal and Mukherjee a 'bigot'! Similarly, Swamy is generally criticised by the liberal establishment as a maverick, a loose cannon, an unguided missile, a muckraker. Senior journalist Ambikanand Sahay wrote in an article on www.firstpost.com: 'Fools rush in where angels fear to tread is an age-old saying – which essentially means that foolish people usually do not understand when a situation is dangerous. Subramanian Swamy fits into this maxim perfectly.'[2]

Evidently, Sahay has no respect for Swamy despite the fact that the Rightwing leader played a heroic role against the Emergency (1975-77), India's brief brush with tyranny after Independence. According to Sahay, 'He is an unguided missile, loose cannon.'

In a similar vein, Rajesh Ramachandran wrote in *The Economic Times* on 1 May 2016 that Swamy'is a muckraker par excellence. He can hurl abuses, he can talk through his hat, attack iconic national leaders and get away with it all.'[3]

Swamy is generally lambasted and lampooned in the mainstream media in India. This is despite the fact he has fought for political liberty and free speech. Leaders like Nehru, however, are often held in high esteem even though they have encroached upon freedom of expression.

Such are the absurdities of India's public discourse.

---

2 Seehttp://www.firstpost.com/world/dear-subramanian-swamy-this-isnt-1999-and-narendra-modi-isnt-vajpayee-2855606.html (25 June 2016)

3 See http://economictimes.indiatimes.com/news/politics-and-nation/how-subramanian-swamy-has-always-managed-to-be-in-the-limelight-through-his-maverick-ways/articleshow/52055943.cms?intenttarget=no

Chapter 5

Expression versus Law & Order

In India, as in other countries, demands are often made for a ban on movies, paintings, books, songs, and other creative works. These demands are accompanied with overt and covert threats: ban it, or else... Apparently sound arguments are made in favour of capitulation. After all, it is just a movie, song, or book; why hurt the sentiments of another; why risk peace and amity in society; why should Law&Order be compromised just because some Johnny thinks that his creation is a great piece of art? At any rate, human lives are more important than art. In facing the above, governments have to consider whether the arguments are justified. If the (easy) answer is yes, the offended (and raucous) group is appeased, the spectre of large-scale violence fades away and the authorities breathe easy.

However, let us takethe tough option and consider why the correct answer should be no: A ban is wrong not only in principle but also as an expedient measure. It is wrong in theory because it violates or curbs the freedom of expression: without citizens' freedom of expression, democracy is reduced to a farce. Democracy is not just about casting a vote and electing representatives for state assemblies and Parliament, it is a way of life: if you can't say what you want to say, it is democratic form, without substance. The principle worth imbibing is an old one: give me liberty or give me death.

Why offend somebody?

It is often argued that freedom of expression does not mean license to offend others. Why must Salman Rushdie write a book that offends the Muslims? After all, he was a writer of repute even before he published *Satanic Verses*; his other books brought critical acclaim and commercial success, so why must he write a blasphemous novel in the first place? Similarly, why must M.F. Husain paint the goddess Saraswati in the nude? Why must Taslima Nasreen write novels which offend the Muslims? Why must the Danish cartoonist sketch the Prophet Mohammad?

But the point is that, as George Orwell said, if liberty means anything at all, it means the right to tell people what they do *not* want to hear. If you tell me that I am a great author and I let you say that, it is neither liberty nor tolerance. You enjoy liberty only if you tell me that my writing is not worth the paper it is printed on; and I am tolerant when, even if I have the power to squash you, I let you express your opinion. And it is genuine democracy if I, however powerful I may be, cannot hurt you for the nasty things you say about me, because the law protects you.

Former US President Ronald Reagan famously cracked a joke at one of his press conferences: An American and a Russian had an argument about freedom of speech in their respective countries. The American said that he could go to White House, enter the Oval Office, and tell the President, 'Mr. Reagan, you are a fool!'

The Russian responded, saying that he could also go to the Kremlin, enter Gorbachev's office, and scream, 'Mr. Gorbachev, Mr. Reagan is a fool!'

Further, it is practically impossible for a creative person to envisage what would offend somebody. Yes, sometimes people say and do things for instant publicity, but that is neither criminal nor immoral so long as it does not hurt others. For instance, how could the makers of the movie, *Billu Barber*, have imagined that the neutral word 'barber', which is not pejorative by any stretch of imagination, would get them into trouble?

The vagaries of political correctness

Finally, if a creative person has to always take the sensibilities of over-sensitive people and the vagaries of political correctness into account, how could he create anything of consequence? He would be busy studying, analysing, and examining the nuances of every word, every epithet, and every utterance.

As for the fears about the worsening of Law & Order situation if 'offensive' books, movies and the like are not banned, one can only say that the fears are grossly exaggerated. This is not to say that there are no fears: Hindu groups have attacked painting exhibitions by M.F. Husain and Jatin Das; Salman Rushdie did receive a fatwa from Iran's Ayatollah Khomeini for his novel *Satanic Verses*. While Rushdie was not physically hurt, many others were.

Hitoshi Igarashi, the Japanese scholar who translated *The Satanic Verses*, was stabbed to death in July 1991. The body of 44-year-old Igarashi, an assistant professor of comparative Islamic culture at Tsukuba University, northeast of Tokyo, had knife wounds in the neck, face, and hands. In the same month, Ettore Capriolo, the translator of the book in Italian, was also knifed, though he survived with injuries on his neck, chest, and hands.

In 1993, there was an assassination attempt on William Nygaard, publisher of the Norwegian edition of *The Satanic Verses*. In the same year, an attempt was also made to kill Aziz Nesin, a Turkish writer who had begun translating the book. Incensed with his boldness, jihadists set the hotel afire in which he was staying. As many as thirty-seven people were roasted alive though Nesin managed to escape.

It is important to note here that since that unfortunate incident, no *Satanic Verses*-related violence has happened in Turkey. The reason: Turkey refused to forget the Sivas Massacre or forgive the perpetrators.

An angry mob of Islamic fundamentalists had attacked the Madımak Hotel in Sivas after traditional Friday prayers. The intellectuals had gathered at the Madımakto celebrate sixteenth century poet Pir Sultan Abdal. The attackers were incensed by the presence of Aziz Nesin, a writer who had translated and published extracts from *Satanic Verses*. While Nesin managed to escape because the mob did not recognise him, dozens perished in the arson attack.

The State Security Court sentenced thirty-three people to death in November 1997 for the massacre. In a 2001 appeal, all but two of these sentences were upheld. The sentences were however commuted to life in prison as Turkey abolished capital punishment in 2002.

Remembering champions of liberty

Civil society organisations and prominent intellectuals every year commemorate the anniversary of the Sivas Massacre. In 2010 the Turkish government, for the first time, joined in ceremonies remembering the outrage which had claimed the lives of many intellectuals, writers, and artists. 'The pain of Madımak is the pain of the entire country,' State Minister Faruk Çelik said at the commemoration ceremony held in front of the Madımak Hotel and attended by other government officials. Çelik went on to call 2 July 1993 one of the most painful dates in Turkish history. 'That day, they wanted to test the brotherhood we have built for centuries, with blood and tears,' he said. He went on to add: 'The fire that encompassed the hotel affected all our bodies.'

What this shows is that the Islamist fundamentalists, despite their bluff and bluster, are mostly a cowardly lot; they become dangerous when they get the impression that they can get away with murder. It also shows that in Turkey, intellectuals actually died and suffered for the cause of the freedom of expression, unlike their counterparts in India who invariably succumb to the pressures of Islamic fundamentalists, and whose fight for freedom of expression is restricted to a tirade against 'fanatic Hindus.'

This is not to say that Hindu groups pose no threat to the freedom of expression. Their campaign against *Shivaji: The Hindu King in Muslim India*, a book written by American scholar James Laine, is a case in point. The book not only occasioned a ban and several court cases but also violence. Shivaji Bhosle (1630-1680), the Maratha Emperor with the royal title *Chhatrapati Shivaji Maharaj*, fought for the freedom of the Maratha nation from the Sultanate of Bijapur. Owing to his fight against the Muslim rulers, including the mighty Mughals, he is a hero of Hindu nationalists. His many adventures have bestowed a halo on this legend. In Maharashtra, he is especially cherished as a cult figure. Local parties like the Shiv Sena, which peddle Maratha pride, almost worship him and even the slightest hint of criticism, let alone disparagement, is projected as blasphemy. The Mumbai (formerly Bombay) airport was renamed as Chhatrapati Shivaji International Airport.

The Shivaji controversy

In June 2003, *Shivaji* was published in India by Oxford University Press India. In November, scholars affiliated with the Bhandarkar Oriental Research Institute (BORI) of Pune, among them MP Pradeep Rawat, demanded the withdrawal of the book. The OUP was prompt in coming out with an apology; it also withdrew the book from the Indian market. This, however, did not appease Shiv Sena activists who, on 22 December, assaulted scholars attached to BORI, for their assistance to Laine for his book. Sanskrit scholar Shrikant Bahulkar was beaten up and his face blackened. A few days later, James Laine faxed a statement, saying:

> It was never my intention to defame the great Maharashtrian hero. I had no desire to upset those for whom he is an emblem of regional and national pride, and I apologise for inadvertently doing so. I foolishly misread the situation in India and figured the book would receive scholarly criticism, not censorship and condemnation. Again I apologise.

The campaign against the book continued, nonetheless. On 5 January 2004, over 150 members of the Sambhaji Brigade ransacked BORI, vandalising the building, books, and artworks. The state government, however, did little to stem the assaults. State home minister R.R. Patil said in *The Indian Express*:

> We condemn the attack and also distorting of the history of Chhatrapati Shivaji. The government is seeking legal opinion to ascertain if any action can be taken against the author and also whether the book can be banned.

Notice the bracketing of scholarship with criminality. Unsurprisingly, the criminals were emboldened. On 9 January, Sambhaji Brigade spokesman Shrimant Kokate is reported to have said in *The Times of India*: 'In fact, scholars should be happy that BORI is still intact.' The brigade was 'most unhappy' that scholars who had helped Laine were 'still alive.' In another report in *The Indian Express*, he was quoted as saying, 'Those who fed him [Laine] with the offensive information should be hanged by the government. If the government is unable to do so, they should be handed over to us.' As for the news persons disapproving of vandalism, Kokate said: 'We will deal with the media later.'

On 14 January, the Maharashtra government proposed to ban the book, citing Sections 153 and 153A of the Indian Penal Code. Two days later, Prime Minister Atal Bihari Vajpayee opposed the proscription, infuriating the ally Shiv Sena. In *The Indian Express* he said:

> If you do not like anything in a particular book, then sit and discuss it. Banning a book is not a solution. We have to tackle it

ideologically... If differences of opinion remain after an issue is discussed, the best way would be to come out with another good book on the subject.

Bans affect all

It must be noted that it was not just the pro-Hindu outfits like the Shiv Sena which were whipping up a frenzy against the book; leaders of other parties also joined in to capitalise on so-called popular sentiments. Senior Congress leader and former Maharashtra chief minister A.R. Antulay castigated Laine and urged the government to take all the necessary legal steps to punish him. In *The Hindu*, Chief minister Sushilkumar Shinde said that it was 'not fair' to write such 'bad things' about Shivaji.

Fortunately, the Bombay High Court decided against the ban; and the Supreme Court on 9 July 2010 upheld the high court's decision. The apex court maintained that the Maharashtra government did not follow the mandatory procedures while invoking the ban on the book.

In the *Shivaji* controversy, politicians saw a golden opportunity to gain popularity by transmogrifying the people into rabble. In what he thought was an excellent exercise in competitive populism, Maharashtra BJP president Gopinath Munde also demanded a ban on Jawaharlal Nehru's book, *Discovery of India*, claiming that a 1986 edition contained derogatory remarks about Shivaji. But he had not read the book; and the hearsay he relied on proved to be misleading. When it was pointed out that no such remarks were found in that edition, he sheepishly said, 'I am a politician and not a scholar.'

The controversy over *Shivaji: The Hindu King in Muslim India* was just one of the many that Hindu groups kicked off. In 1998, they unleashed hell against Deepa Mehta's film *Fire* on the grounds that it portrayed a distorted version of Indian society. The movie was about a lesbian relationship between two family members. On 2 December 1988 activists of the Shiv Sena Mahila Aghadi attacked the matinee show of the film at Cinemax theatre in suburban Goregaon in Mumbai. Glass panes were smashed, posters burnt and slogans raised against the movie.

A day later, women stormtroopers vandalised Regal Cinema in the heart of the national Capital, accompanied by TV camera crews. The cops, however, were conspicuous by their absence. *Fire* producer Bobby Bedi was quoted in *India Today* as saying: 'The Delhi Sena chief's letter informing the press about the demonstration said that they would do *tod-phod* [vandalism] and violence was expected… almost as if tea will be served.' Pune was next, then Surat.

According to *India Today*:

> On the eve of their attack on Cinemax, the Mahila Aghadi women called on state Culture Minister Pramod Navalkar to protest against the depiction of the 'lesbian relationship' between Shabana Azmi and Nandita Das in the film. They even demand Azmi's resignation from the Rajya Sabha.

While Navalkar obviously gave the green light, Chief Minister Manohar Joshi egged them on, while patting them on their backs. 'I congratulate them for what they have done. The film's theme is alien to our culture,' said Joshi on the day the Sainiks attacked cinema halls and succeeded in stopping a film cleared by the Censor Board. Of course, Joshi backed down later saying he was only supporting their protest and not the vandalism.

The charge of the Sena brigade was however successful: Union Minister of State for Information & Broadcasting M.A. Naqvi, sent *Fire* back to the Censor Board. Once approved, a film is rarely referred back to the censors, with exceptions like R.V. Pandit's *Maachis* [directed by Gulzar] because of its supposed soft treatment of terrorists. You need a 'public outrage' for that. And the Sena obliged.

There is a pattern here, of course. The bodies protesting against a work of art are front organisations of the Sangh Parivar or the Shiv Sena. The pro-Hindu political parties are under the (false) impression that a sanctimonious thump over 'the great and glorious Indian culture' will bring in a rich harvest of votes. As Manohar Joshi's flirtation with the activists indicated, the vandals enjoy political and administrative support. It is clear, therefore, that the real threat to Law & Order does not emanate from the artists' flights of fancy but from politicians' shielding of hooligans.

Discerning the pattern

It is not just the Bharatiya Janata Party and the Shiv Sena, but also the Congress and other 'secular' or 'liberal' parties which have great faith in stormtroopers. The grand old party, in a bid to outsmart the regionalism and sectarianism of the mainstream Akalis, set up Bhindranwale, resulting in the assassination of Prime Minister Indira Gandhi and killing of thousands of people of all faiths. Similarly, to counter the Maratha chauvinism of the Shiv Sena, it propped up Maharashtra Navnirman Sena Chief Raj Thackeray, and refused to take action against the violence he wrought. Trinamool Congress chief Mamata Banerjee's effort to outwit the Marxists in West Bengal plays out on similar lines; she has partnered with the ruthless Maoists.

Clearly it is the shortsightedness of mainstream politicians that creates Law & Order problems, not the works of art, however outrageous these works might be. If the vandals are brought to justice and the rule of law is upheld, there would be no lawlessness and disruptions in the public space.

Chapter 6

How censor board and others torment filmmakers

Technically, there is no film censor in India. There is a Central Board of Film Certification (CBFC) which, according to its website, 'is a Statutory body under Ministry of Information and Broadcasting, regulating the public exhibition of films under the provisions of the Cinematograph Act 1952.' In reality, it is the country's censor board—an obnoxious and odious one to boot. Not quitea benign organisation, it earned a lot of notoriety when Prime Minister Narendra Modi appointed Pahlaj Nihalani, famous for making forgettable movies, as CBFC Chairman in January 2015. I will discuss Nihalani later in this chapter. More important is a discussion on the instrumentality that curbs filmmakers' freedom in the first place: the CBFC's mission and guidelines.

In India, films can be publicly exhibited only after they have been certified by the CBFC. The Board comprises non-official members and a chairman. All of them are appointed by the federal government. Headquartered in Mumbai, the Board has nine regional offices, one each in Mumbai, Kolkata, Chennai, Bangalore, Thiruvananthapuram, Hyderabad, New Delhi, Cuttack, and Guwahati. Every office is assisted by advisory panels in the examination of films. The members of these panels are nominated by the federal government for a period of two years by drawing people from different walks of life.

Films are certified under four categories: 'U' certificate or Unrestricted Public Exhibition; 'UA' certificate or Unrestricted Public Exhibition but with a word of caution that parental discretion is required for children below twelve years; 'A' certificate or restricted to adults; and 'S' certificate or restricted to any special class of persons. The certification process is in accordance with the Cinema to graph Act 1952, the Cinema to graph (certification) Rules 1983, and the guidelines issued by the Central government, according to the official website. The CBFC's mission is: 'To ensure the good and healthy entertainment in accordance with the provisions of the Cinematograph Act 1952 and the Cinematograph (Certification) Rules 1983.' It is also mandated, among other things, 'to ensure... education to the public.'

The guidelines firmly establish that the CBFC is not just a certification body but the censor board. Quoting the Cinematograph Act, its website says that 'a film shall not be certified if any part of it is against the interest of the sovereignty and integrity of India, the security of the State, friendly relations with foreign States, public order, decency or involves defamation or contempt of court or is likely to incite commission of any offence.' This is in accordance with the reasonable restrictions on the right to freedom of expression as prescribed in the Constitution.

The guidelines are an elaborate exercise in pontification, ambiguity, and moral policing. 'A film is judged in its entirety from the point of view of its overall impact and is examined in the light of the period depicted in the film and the contemporary standards of the country and the people to whom the film relates, provided that the film does not deprave the morality of the audience. Guidelines are applied to the titles of the films also.' That's for starters.

One of the objectives, the guidelines say, is that the medium of film should remain 'responsible and sensitive to the values and standards of society.' What about a filmmaker who rebels against the society, who finds its values and standards sickening? And what are the values and standards of society anyway? There are caste *panchayats* (village councils) which refuse to come out of the seventeenth century. Then there are men and women who have imbibed the ideals and values of modernity. And there are postmodern activists, LGBT advocates, *etc.* So, whose standards and whose values?

Another objective is that 'the medium of film provides clean and healthy entertainment.' What's that? Nobody knows. The Dev Anand starrer *Guide*, which some people say is the best Hindi movie ever made, is about a married Christian woman eloping with a Hindu man. The man smokes, drinks, and gets convicted in a cheating case. It may be a great movie but the adjectives 'clean' and 'healthy' can scarcely be used either for the content or the characters. The same applies to Guru Dutt's *Sahib, Bibi aur Ghulam*, another classic that depicts the debauchery and decadence of feudalism.

The CBFC insists that 'anti-social activities such as violence are not glorified or justified' and 'the modus operandi of criminals, other visuals or words likely to incite the commission of any offence are not depicted.' Further, filmmakers are not supposed to show scenes 'showing involvement of children in violence as victims or perpetrators or as forced witnesses to violence, or showing children as being subjected to any form of child abuse.'

But the modus operandi of criminals is often described in great detail in the media. Should that too be banned? Similarly, crimes by juveniles and child abuse are presented in newspapers and TV channels. Should there be any restrictions on such presentation? The 2016 release *Kahaani 2* starring Vidya Balan, deals with the taboo subject of pedophilia and incest. Had any CBFC boss put up a protest, the movie could have been banned, by virtue of the above-mentioned provision.

Other CBFC guidelines include: abuse or ridicule of physically and mentally handicapped persons; showing cruelty to, or abuse of animals, are not presented needlessly; pointless or avoidable scenes of violence, cruelty, and horror, scenes of violence primarily intended to provide entertainment and such scenes as may have the effect of de-sensitising or de-humanising people; scenes which have the effect of justifying or glorifying drinking; scenes tending to encourage, justify or glamorise drug addiction; scenes tending to encourage, justify or glamorise consumption of tobacco or smoking.

But what is the film director expected to show when the storyline includes loutish, uncouth characters who indulge in body shaming: when the story is about a pervert involved in bestiality; when it is about violent and cruel characters; when characters, even protagonists, actually glory vices? In the Bimal Roy classic (1956), *Devdas*, there is a famous Dilip Kumar dialogue: *Kaun kambakht hai jo bardasht karne ke liye peeta hai, main to peeta hoon ke bas saans le sakoon* (Who the heck drinks to suffer the consequences! I drink just to stay alive). I doubt if this scene would pass muster with a Nihalani at the CBFC helm.

Nobody in the right state of mind justifies—at least publicly—body shaming, bestiality, violence, desensitisation or dehumanisation, smoking, alcohol consumption, substance abuse, and other vices. But these things do exist in society; and cinema, like any other art, reflects reality. The dharma and the karma of a movie director are to create works of art to the best of his ability; getting the society rid of its sins is beyond his remit.

But the tribalist, collectivist mindset has gone berserk in India; it wants everything and everybody to conform to its basic principle: the society, the nation, or some other collectivity is of supreme importance and, concomitantly, the individual has no importance in his own right; whatever value can be ascribed to him is because of his utility to the collectivity he is supposed to serve; the collectivity is everything, the individual is nothing. And since the filmmaker, among all creative persons, has the maximum reach, he has to be kept on a short leash. It is interesting to note in this context that in novels, short stories, and other forms of literature, one can write practically anything without disclaimers. The reason is simple: not many people read in India.

But everybody watches movies, so directors should ideally come up with films that give some 'message' to society; they should make 'socially relevant' movies. But if they are so dumb as to not realise their duty, at least they should not be allowed to spoil the morals of people at large. This is the mindset behind Talibansque regulation of cinema.

The CBFC guidelines not only tend to chastise the rebellious, unruly movie directors but also promote political correctness and sanctimoniousness. Therefore, the filmmaker has to ensure that:

> human sensibilities are not offended by vulgarity, obscenity or depravity; such dual meaning words as obviously cater to baser instincts are not allowed; scenes degrading or denigrating women in any manner are not presented; scenes involving sexual violence against women like attempt to rape, rape or any form of molestation or scenes of a similar nature are avoided, and if any such incidence is germane to the theme, they shall be reduced to the minimum and no details are shown; scenes showing sexual perversions shall be avoided and if such matters are germane to the theme they shall be reduced to the minimum and no details are shown; visuals or words contemptuous of racial, religious or other groups are not presented: visuals or

words which promote communal, obscurantist, anti-scientific and anti-national attitude are not presented.

There are several objections to this set of homilies. First, non-depiction of depravity, obscenity, double entendre, degradation of women, rape, sexual perversions, obscurantism, *etc.,* in movies would not end them. Second, there are no objective standards to determine what is, say, obscenity or obscurantism. Is *Lady Chatterley's Lover* obscene? Is the rape scene in *Bandit Queen*, with its raw violence, worthy of depiction on screen? Are astrology-based television programmes obscurantist? There are no universally accepted answers to these questions.

Third, CBFC guidelines reveal their overreach mentality. CBFC should restrict its role to its primary responsibility: film certification. Social reform, women uplift, spread of scientific temperament, and other such laudable objectives are beyond its purview.

Fourth, scenes of depravity, sexual violence, drug use, religious hatred, *etc.*, are not endorsements of such abominations; more often than not, such depiction is intended to highlight the evil of these activities. The 2015 film, *Udta Punjab*, against which Nihalani almost waged a jihad, was full of swear words, substance abuse, sexual violence, depravity, *etc.*, but it was against them, not justifying or glorifying them.

Fifthly, the CBFC guidelines are an affront to the rule of law: sometimes, the men and women heading the body follow the guidelines, sometimes they don't. There is the uber-reactionary Nihalani, but there was also the great Vijay Anand. The director of Guide and other classics, he once was the CBFC chief. At that time, he recommended that adult films should be allowed to be screened in special, strictly-supervised theatres. The then Minister of Information &Broadcasting Sushma Swaraj, another reactionary, rejected the idea; he quit. 'There were rumors that the proposal was scuttled by the cash-rich blue film video exhibitor lobby,' *The Hindu* reported on 5 March 2004, in Anand's obituary.

Finally, and most importantly, the homilies severely curtail the freedom of expression of movie directors, as they also limit the choice of viewers. If the CBFC's list of proscriptions is strictly adhered to, filmmakers would be forced to pick up bland storylines—strictly *sanskari* stuff, bland family dramas, slapstick comedies, *et al.* The viewers would be left with insipid stories. It will be the demise of creativity as well as of recreation. ('*Sanskar*', noun, is practically untranslatable in English.

It may mean 'value,' 'sacrament,' 'ritual,' 'investiture,' 'refinement,' or 'religious disposition.' '*Sanskari*' is the adjective. It is widely used to lampoon sanctimonious Hindus. Typically, Nihalani brazened out his insolence, saying, 'I don't mind being called *sanskari* if it is in the national interest').

Nihalani has always believed in implementing the guidelines in letter and spirit. In February 2015—that is, soon after becoming CBFC chief—he came up with a list of cuss words which he ordered to be removed from any movie that came up to his board for certification. It had Hindi and English words, including 'bastard' and its Hindi version '*haraamzaada*,' 'screw,' 'asshole,' 'son of a bitch,' and various Indian translations of 'bitch,' *etc*. His was an exercise in rightwing political correctness—and a perverse assault on the freedom of expression. Such was the extent of perversity that even the Right-leaning CBFC members, Ashoke Pandit and Chandraprakash Dwivedi, criticised him in no uncertain terms. Nihalani, however, was undeterred by that. He issued a fatwa restricting the duration of Daniel Craig-Monica Bellucci kiss in the James Bond movie *Spectre*. Nihalani didn't just want to save our morals but also wanted to shield children from anything scary, so he gave *The Jungle Book* a U/A certificate.

The makers of *Dum Laga Ke Haisha*, a family entertainer, had to excise four words, including 'lesbian'. *Prem Ratan Dhan Payo*, from a production house known for movies promoting family values, had to do away with a word *rakhail*(mistress). Further, they had to cut out a Ram-Leela scene from the film.[4] The CBFC ordered eleven cuts in *Jai Gangaajal*, directed by Prakash Jha, starring Priyanka Chopra. This was reduced to two by the Film Certification Appellate Tribunal (FCAT). Jha accused Nihalani of 'personal agenda' and 'manipulations'.

In Badlapur, Nihalani ordered the removal of a scene where Varun Dhawan strangulates Nawazuddin. *NH10* was produced by the actress Anushka Sharma: the CBFC didn't allow the word *randi* (whore) to be uttered. The sex comedy, *Kya Kool Hai Hum 3*, was ordered over a 100 cuts; even *popat* (parrot) was not allowed. The movie *Shaandaar*that turned out to be a flop, also had considerable trouble with the board.

4 According to www.firstpost.com (http://www.firstpost.com/bollywood/cuts-like-a-razor-a-list-of-the-most-bizzare-acts-of-censorship-by-pahlaj-nihalani-2824666.html).

There are many more instances of Nihalani and other CBFC bosses playing spoilsports. To a votary of liberty, all this seems to be sanctimony- and reaction-induced insanity, but there may be method in this madness. As in the arena of economic policy, bad decisions often lead to myriad problems for stakeholders and, consequently, corruption. By the time the attention of a decent politician or policymaker is attracted towards the issue, many vested interests get entrenched, and often they acquire a life of their own.

The film certification process in India may have followed the pattern. There is at least one solid accusation of venality. In August 2014, the Central Bureau of Investigation arrested CBFC Chief Executive Officer Rakesh Kumar in an alleged bribery case. The agency also arrested an authorised censor agent and an advisory panel member of the CBFC for demanding a Rs 70,000 bribe on behalf of the CEO to urgently clear a film from Chhattisgarh,' reported *The Times of India*on 18 August 2014.

A 1997-batch Indian Railway Personnel Service officer, Kumar was accused of 'allegedly delaying to issue the film Censor certificates to put pressure on producers to bribe him.' This case may be the tip of the iceberg, for several film personalities complain about corruption in the CBFC. A member of a CBFC advisory panelsays that in every region, there is a set of agents who act as mediators between filmmakers and officials. He recounts stories about the pigheadedness and incredible stupidity of some CBFC panel members, many of whom are there because of their unflinching devotion to Prime Minister Modi. One of them objected to the reference to poverty in a movie. The Modi-*bhakta*'s (Modi-worshipper's) objection was that since the ascension of Modi in May 2014, poverty has vanished from the country, so the reference is an affront to the nation!

However, Modi-*bhaktas* alone are not the enemies of cinema. The Transport Department of Uttar Pradesh, India's largest state, wanted to ban car chases in movies. According to a report in *DNA* on 17 July2015:

> Uttar Pradesh Transport Department has directed district magistrates of the state to impose a ban on scenes in commercials, television series or films that portray violation of traffic rules. According to the transport commissioner, K. Ravindra Naik, such scenes tend to influence public,

> especially youth, in violating traffic rules and encourage them for rash and drunken driving.[5]

The UP Transport Commissioner directed the state's district magistrates 'to monitor content and ensure that stunt scenes in commercials and movies that show over speeding, drunken driving and doing stunts on bikes or riding two wheelers without wearing helmets be banned.' Notice the preposterousness and ludicrousness of the situation: the top transport official of one of the poorly governed states is not as much bothered about *real* overspeeding, rash and drunken driving, and the general flouting of traffic rules, as he is about such acts in movies.

Ideas may have ruled the world, but in India bad ideas are regnant. Soon after UP's notification, the Telangana government came up with a similar fiat. *The Telegraph* of Kolkata reported on 1 October 2015:

> The Telangana government is thinking of banning all chase scenes involving motorbikes, cars and speedboats in films, as a possible antidote to real-life speed racing. The government says many youths have died while imitating or practising 'such stunts' on empty streets or highways.[6]

It issued a notification to film chambers of commerce and associations of producers, directors and actors that all scenes of chase involving motorbikes, cars and speedboats would be censored. 'All such stunts are leading to deaths of innocent youth(s)...' it was averred. In fact, even the Central government toyed with the idea of checking, if not banning, car chases in movies but thankfully, it was not pursued very seriously.

In a nutshell, politicians, activists, publicity-seekers, extortionists, carpetbaggers, and charlatans try to shackle filmmakers under one pretext or the other. The CBFC often plays ball with them.

---

5 See http://www.dnaindia.com/locality/gautam-buddha-nagar/transport-dept-seeks-get-rash-driving-scenes-ads-films-banned-64904.

6 See http://www.telegraphindia.com/1151001/jsp/nation/story_45538.jsp.WELoeBp961u.

Chapter 7

Film censorship and the law of inexorability

We discussed in the last chapter that in India no other form of human expression has faced more restrictions than cinema. This is not surprising as more people watch movies than they read books. Unfortunately, it is not only the Central Board of Film Certification (CBFC) which does the job of censorship, but a variety of forces tend to curtail the creative freedom of filmmakers.

Justification for censorship

Why should cinema be subjected to censorship when other forms of expression like the press, novels, and short stories are not? The Supreme Court of India justified film censorship arguing:

> Film censorship becomes necessary because a film motivates thought and action and assures a high degree of attention and retention as compared to the printed word. The combination of act and speech, sight and sound in semi darkness of the theatre with elimination of all distracting ideas will have a strong impact on the minds of the viewers and can affect emotions. Therefore, it has as much potential for evil as it has for good and has an equal

> potential to instill or cultivate violent or good behavior. It cannot be equated with other modes of communication. Censorship by prior restraint is, therefore, not only desirable but also necessary.

The argument that a movie has 'a strong impact on the minds of the viewers and can affect emotions' is predicated on the notion that the minds of free citizens need to be quarantined from potential viruses that may 'instill or cultivate violent or good behavior.' According to that logic, every book, newspaper, television programme, *etc.*, should be censored.

Now, even if the apparently harmless vision of the CBFC (good and healthy entertainment) and the apex court's justification (potential for evil) are accepted at face value, it is not possible to resolve the issue, for there have been instances where films have been banned despite a clearance from the censor board. While categorising films into various certificates as mentioned above, is essential, the very idea of CBFC acting as a censor board is far from laudable. What makes matters worse is that the CBFC certification is not considered final either by the political class or by society.

Mrinal Sen's film *Neel Akasher Neechey* (1959) was banned for two years, apparently by the government and not the censor board. That it was banned by the government of Jawaharlal Nehru, supposedly a champion of liberty, makes the assault on creative freedom even more intriguing and deplorable. His government also went on to proscribe the 1962 film *Nine Hours to Rama*, which showed Nathuram Godse's political and psychological motivation for killing Gandhi. The movie was based on a book by celebrated historian Stanley Wolpert; the man who also wrote an authoritative biography of Nehru.

Lesser politicians who came later, showed much less tolerance to the subjects and viewpoints they considered unpalatable. Directed by Gulzar *Aandhi* (1975), it was said to be based on the relationships between Indira Gandhi, Nehru, and Feroze Gandhi. Its release faced problems even though it showed Indira Gandhi in a favourable light. There was also Amrit Nahata's film *Kissa Kursi Ka* (1977). Though not depicting any prominent leader in particular, it showed a corrupt and vile politician wooing the public. The movie was banned by the government.

A nation's pique

Nationalistic peevishness also played its role. In 1984, *Indiana Jones and the Temple of Doom* was proscribed for the 'racist portrayal of Indians and overt imperialistic tendencies.' The West Bengal government banned *City of Joy* in 1992 for the alleged denigration of Calcutta.

Prudery has also been the bane of filmmakers. *Kama Sutra: A Tale of Love Banned* (1996) faced trouble with the censors; a truncated version was later released. The same year, *Fire* faced the ire of Hindu groups who objected to lesbianism and the names of protagonists Sita and Radha. Using these names for lesbians was mischievous, the activists said, and a slur on Hinduism. Religious sensibilities are easily offended in India. Politicians in some states with a substantial Christian population banned *The Da Vinci Code*, even though the largely Christian West did not.

Sometimes it is hunger for publicity that propels people to attacks films. The 2009 *Billu Barber* met with fierce resistance from salon and beauty parlour associations; they said that 'barber' was derogatory. The head of the film's production company, Shahrukh Khan, was forced to rename it *Billu*. He also invited members of the Hairdressers's Association of Mumbai to the première of the movie in order to placate them.

Politics have always played a big role in attracting proscription. In 1971, Satyajit Ray's film *Sikkim* faced a ban, which lasted till September 2010. In 2006, the film *Fanaa* was banned in Gujarat for a strange reason—the lead star, Aamir Khan, was against the Sardar Sarovar Dam built over the River Narmada and had demanded adequate rehabilitation for the ousted villagers. Shatrughan Sinha, popular film star and member of the Bharatiya Janata Party (which ruled in the state), even hinted that his party would launch violent protests if Khan did not retract his support to the anti-dam activists. Then there was the curious case of *Jo Bole So Nihal*. In May 2005, the Shiromani Akali Dal (SAD) sought a ban on the film in which the hero, Sunny Deol, played the role of a Sikh cop. 'The producer of the film has misused the holy Sikh community slogan (*Bole So Nihal*),' SAD chief Parkash Singh Badal told a press conference. And yet, 'It is pertinent to mention here that a sub-committee of the Akal Takht had given a "clean chit" to the Hindi film starring Sunny Deol,' said a PTI report on 18 May.

The ruckus was the product of intra-Akali bickering; some factions used the movie as a pretext to score brownie points. A later controversy, regarding the ban on Prakash Jha's film *Aarakshan*, was a typical case of political correctness not just going berserk, but also revealing the shenanigans of politicians.

The chairman of National Commission for Scheduled Castes & Scheduled Tribes, P.L. Punia, objected to some dialogues in the film, calling them anti-Dalit (Dalits, who are called Scheduled Castes in official terminology, are the sections of Hindu society which were discriminated against for centuries; worse, the discrimination had religious sanction). This was despite the fact that the film was cleared by a panel comprising nine people, including a Dalit activist and a former high court judge. Usually such panels include four or five people.

The result of Punia's intractability was that the movie was banned in Uttar Pradesh, Andhra Pradesh, and Punjab.

Politics, plain and simple

It was politics, pure and simple, of course. Punia, a Congress leader who was earlier a confidante of Uttar Pradesh chief minister Mayawati, wanted to present himself as a 'true' leader of the Dalits. The Congress and Mayawati's Bahujan Samaj Party, seen as big rivals in the country's largest state, were both vying for the bigger chunk of the Dalit vote. It was Jha's misfortune that he was caught in the crossfire.

Rajneeti, another film by Jha, also faced trouble because the lead character played by Katrina Kaif, resembled the life of Congress chief Sonia Gandhi—or so the Congress activists claimed.

More dangerous than the machinations of politicians is the tacit and often explicit support they get from intellectuals in the assault on freedom of expression. For instance, Dalit scholar Kancha Ilaiah and prominent journalist Ajay Bose practically supported the ban on *Aarakshan*. Bose saw nothing wrong with Mayawati's ban on *Aarakshan,* indicating that she was entitled to take whatever action she deemed fit for her political survival; any action for political survival was presented as if it were violence in self-defence, which is not illegal. The ideals and rights enshrined in the Constitution mattered little to Bose.

It is this intellectual milieu that emboldens the political class to trample upon the fundamental rights of citizens. Eminent academics, media Brahmins, and other opinion makers—most of them steeped in a regressive mindset—have convinced themselves that meaningful change in human existence can be brought about only by the state. A natural corollary is that any political machination is justified; hence the condoning of the actions of Punia and Mayawati by the intellectuals.

In summary, the so-called reasonable restrictions on the freedom of expression may have occasioned the censor board to regulate cinema but the matter did not end there. As every other government regulation, it has also acquired a life of its own, often making the existence of the CBFC redundant. Any political party, social outfit, cultural group, or publicity seeker can don the mantle of a censor and torment a filmmaker. Punia put forth reasonable restrictions to justify his attack on *Aarakshan*; it is another matter that the restrictions he wanted to impose were unreasonable. The concept from which the censor board derives its legitimacy is also the one from which extra-constitutional super-censors derive theirs.

Creative freedom will remain constrained and restrained till the individual is deprived of the right to express himself without restrictions, reasonable or otherwise. Until that is done, grumpy politicians, tetchy outfits, blackmailers, mischief mongers, and troublemakers will inexorably continue to thrive at the expense of freedom of expression.

Chapter 8

Nannies and grannies of all ages

Do everything that you shouldn't be doing, and don't do anything that you should—this seems to have become the guiding principle of governance in India. As if the Ministry of Health & Family Welfare (MoHFW) had done everything in its jurisdiction to ensure wellness for the people, it came up with the illiberal provision of restraining the depiction of tobaccouse on television in November 2011.

The ministry stipulated on 14 November 2011, that in the movies and programmes showing tobacco use, there should be 'anti-tobacco health spots or messages of minimum thirty seconds duration each at the beginning and middle of the film or the television programme.' Also, there should be 'anti-tobacco health warning as a prominent scroll at the bottom of the screen during the period of such display.'

For new movies and TV programmes to have smoking scenes, the official fatwa was even more stringent. The filmmakers and programme producers have to provide, among other things, 'a strong editorial justification for display of tobacco products or their use shall be given to Central Board of Film Certification (CBFC).' Further, the new rules call for a representative of the MoHFW in the CBFC.

The MoHFW diktat severely undermined the freedom of expression as well as the freedom of choice. There are said to be more than twenty-five crore smokers in India, which is over twenty per cent of the country's population. The new rules intend to almost banish one out of five citizens from cinema and television, the two most popular mass media. The stipulation flies in the face of the prevalent governance mantra of 'inclusiveness.'

Besides, there are cult figures that cannot be conceived without tobacco use. Can you show Churchill without a cigar and Sherlock Holmes without his pipe? Can you authentically depict a henchman in Bihar without *khaini*? Can there be a documentary on Albert Camus without a cigarette? Imagine Dev Anand gambling without a cigarette and Clark Gable as Rhett Butler without a cigar! Further, the new rules further restricted the sphere of liberty for creative people. As it is, they are forced to be come up with sanitised works; they are always conscious about words, characters, storylines, themes, *etc.,* lest some tetchy group or downright publicity-seeker come up with an objection that the movie or TV serial 'hurt the sentiments of…' Now, they have to be deferential to the MoHFW commissars as well.

Implicit in the rules is the belief that the people of India are not intelligent or prudent enough to be left unguided at any point of time. It is enough to tell an adult what could be dangerous, so there are verbal and pictorial warnings on the tobacco merchandise. Then there are social messages on radio and television informing the public about the ill effects of tobacco. This implies that the nanny state suspects the cognitive ability of the citizens; it treats them as subjects who should be subjected to relentless haranguing about what is right and what is not, rather than responsible human beings who can take their own decisions.

Hence the incongruity is that a person who is considered sensible enough to elect the government, to become an Indian Administrative Service or Indian Police Service officer, or a general in the Army, is also simultaneously assumed to be so dumb as to need constant reminders about the health hazards of tobacco. Our political masters and even nastier activists are not satisfied with regular warnings on packets; they want to drill into the minds of people that tobacco is bad (and, if possible, program the mind to behave properly), almost in the fashion in which children were brought up in the 1932 novel, *Brave New World*, where phrases are repeated thousands of times while the children sleep in Aldous Huxley's dystopia.

The contradictions inherent in the nanny state are blatantly obvious. Its exchequer receives thousands of crores in taxes from the tobacco industry, even as it campaigns fanatically against tobacco use. Then there is an element of subsidy involved in tobacco farming. The MoHFW shows sanctimonious concern regarding tobacco use, but it does little to combat the far bigger dangers the society has been facing for quite some time. One of them is counterfeit medicines. While a report by the Organisation for Economic Cooperation and Development says that three-quarter of the world's total supply of counterfeit drugs can be traced to India, the World Health Organisation figure is lower, at thirty-five per cent. As for the prevalence of fake drugs in India, some estimates go as high as twenty-five per cent, though there are wide variations in them.

Then there is the issue of food adulteration. Over the years, the problem has worsened. One example is the comparatively recent phenomenon of 'synthetic milk,' which is a concoction made of chemicals such as urea, caustic soda, cheap cooking oil, and detergents. The authorities have done little, if anything, to eradicate this menace, but their concern in some matters is pathological. The issue of mandatory scroll on smoking scenes in cinema and TV progammes is one of them.

We shall begin with the freedom of expression. Article 19 of the Indian Constitution provides:

> Protection of certain rights regarding freedom of speech, etc.—
>
> (1) All citizens shall have the right—
> (a) to freedom of speech and expression.
>
> This Right is subjected to 'reasonable restrictions' which are spelled out as:
>
> 'Nothing in sub-clause (a) of clause (1) shall affect the operation of any existing law, or prevent the State from making any law, in so far as such law imposes reasonable restrictions on the exercise of the right conferred by the said sub-clause in the interests of the sovereignty and integrity of India, the security of the State, friendly relations with foreign States, public order, decency or morality, or in relation to contempt of court, defamation or incitement to an offence.

Evidently, the depiction of a person smoking in cinema screen or on television is neither a threat to 'the sovereignty and integrity of India, the security of the State, friendly relations with foreign States, public order'; nor, by any stretch of imagination, can it be considered 'contempt of court, defamation or incitement to an offence.' Smoking may be regarded as indecent and immoral by some people, but that cannot be a ground to ban or restrict its depiction onscreen, for there are many things which are indecent and immoral, but legitimately find expression in art as they are part of life—and art reflects life.

In 2013, film director Woody Allen didn't release *Blue Jasmine* in India because he refused to insert the scroll. A year earlier, David Fincher's *The Girl With the Dragon Tattoo* could not be released for the same reason. They were foreign filmmakers and could afford to ignore the Indian market, but Indian filmmakers have to bow to the diktats of the government. The mandatory scroll also falls under the rubric of 'spurious goods and services' as defined by the Consumers Protection Act, 1986—that is, 'such goods and services which are claimed to be genuine but they are actually not so.'

The movie that I watch is not genuine if there is a scroll running on any part of the screen at any given point of time. If I pay for the movie, I want my entertainment to be pure, unblemished by any message. Watching a movie with anti-smoking messages is like buying adulterated food. This is evidently the least of government concernsas is action against fake drugs and food adulteration. This is despite the fact that the people involved in such unconscionable practices are simply mass murderers. There is, however, an effort to keep creative people on a short leash, and subject the citizenry to an existence defined by prescriptions and proscriptions. The nannies, grannies, and fogeys of all ages are having a gala time.

Chapter 9

Hurting the sentiments-I

There are two questions few people ask in India: Can offending the feelings or 'hurting the sentiments' be grounds for the proscription of a work of art or a history book, among others? Secondly, are bans enforced in consonance with the law of the land?

In our country, when somebody cries that their sentiments have been hurt because of some movie, song, book, *etc.*, public intellectuals start debating whether there is any merit in the protests. Did the artist or author actually do something offensive? Were sentiments really hurt? Were the demands made for a ban, just?

Let's look at the real question show valid are the demands based on hurt sentiments and how legitimate are the grounds on which various works have been banned, from a legal point of view. As we mentioned earlier, the Indian Constitution imposes 'reasonable restrictions' on the fundamental right to freedom of expression.

Really reasonable?

'Reasonable restrictions' appended to the Right to Freedom of Speech and Expression in Article 19 (a) empowered the State to curb this fundamental right whenever it wished. Restrictions can be imposed for the maintenance of 'the security of the State, friendly relations with foreign States, public order, decency or morality, or in relation to contempt of court, defamation or incitement to an offence.'

Even as I consider the First Amendment to the Indian Constitution an affront to democracy, the restrictions it imposes on free speech are themselves purported to be 'reasonable'. In other words, these can be imposed only if there are *reasonable* grounds for harming national security, jeopardising friendly relations with foreign countries, disturbing public order, offending decency or morality, contemning court, leading to defamation or occasioning incitement to an offence. Nowhere is it mentioned that hurting the sentiments of somebody can be a ground for the curtailment of the freedom of expression. At any rate, reason is often at variance with sentiments.

The grounds restricting the freedom of expression have to be reasonable and *not sentimental*, not only because it is the Constitutional position but also because reasons can be objectively debated, while sentiments can't be. Merriam-Webster describes 'sentiment' as 'an attitude, thought, or judgment prompted by feeling,' 'predilection', 'a specific view or notion,' 'opinion,' 'an idea colored by emotion,' *etc*. It is crystal clear that the defining feature of sentiments is subjectivity.

The law and public administration, on the other hand, are moulded by objective realities. Poetry is to sentiments and subjectivity what political philosophy is to statecraft, jurisprudence, and objectivity. Plato said in the *Republic* that there is an old quarrel between philosophy and poetry. According to him, if poetry is allowed in its ideal state, 'not law and the reason of mankind, which by common consent have ever been deemed best, but pleasure and pain will be the rulers in our state.' This was the reason that he banished poets from his ideal state.

Politics and poetry

In India, however, the dominant principles of polity are poetic in nature. It is not surprising that sentimentality and sanctimoniousness, those illegitimate children of poetry, figure highly in the manifestoes, speeches, statements, and announcements of political parties. Leaders of all hues claim to be concerned about and working for the poor, farmers, and weaker sections of society. They unctuously champion the causes of poverty alleviation, inclusion, food security, health for all, and so on. Yet the policies they chalk out and the way these are implemented result in huge wastage and graft; the beneficiaries are almost invariably politicians and their hangers-on. They ensure that the core of public discourse remains poetic, that reason and empirical evidence do not challenge the ruling dogmas of the big state and a perverted secularism. To this end, they employ various tools and techniques.

To begin with, they install their people in the areas which shape public opinion—higher educational institutions (Jawaharlal Nehru University in Delhi is an example), academia, media *etc*. Secondly, thought crimes are defined as per convenience and severely punished. 'Communalism' is the most heinous thought crime. In plain English, it means anything that is evenly vaguely critical of Islam; even criticism of jihadist terror and Pakistani sometimes attracts the accusation of communal tendencies. Thirdly, *argumentum ad hominem*—that is, attacking the arguer rather than his arguments—is used with devastating effect. So when there is a demand for a uniform civil code, which is also enshrined in the Directive Principles of the Constitution, it is slammed as a means to undermine Islam and secularism in India; even the BJP, which earlier used to call for this modern code, does not talk about it nowadays. Such is the danger of *ad hominem* attacks. Economic reforms are equated with benefits for big industry. Opening up of the country for foreign direct investment is castigated as a treacherous, if not traitorous, design to invite the avatars of the East India Company. Privatisation of public sector undertakings is compared with the selling of the family silver to pay the grocer's bill. Rationalisation of subsidies is denounced as an anti-poor measure. Anybody questioning the wisdom of expanding caste-based reservations is flayed for being anti-Dalit, anti-backward, Manuwadi. Long is the list of *ad hominem* targets, indeed.

The upshot is that reason and informed arguments have taken a back seat in public discourse. It is sentimentalism all the way.

Like malfunctioning robots

Without the ballasts of rationality, poise, and gravitas, sentiments behave like malfunctioning robots; fortuitous combinations of circuits make their working arbitrary and often dangerous. More than any universal ideal of democracy like liberty and fairness, 'pleasure and pain' have become the guiding principles of Indian democracy. As I see it, pleasure and pain include the basest human instincts, grossest emotions, and weirdest ideas; they also include a predilection to capitulate to the cantankerous and the intractable; and they inevitably result in compromises with self-righteous charlatans and pious goons, all in the name of not hurting the sentiments. The biggest casualty, of course, is the freedom of expression.

Let us consider a few cases. *Great Soul: Mahatma Gandhi and His Struggle With India*, a biography authored by Joseph Lelyveld, was banned in Gujarat in 2011. The book suggested that Gandhi had a homosexual relationship. It did not have any repercussions on national security, India's friendly relations with other countries, public order, *etc*. Decency and morality are not in more peril here than they are from the many books on the sexual relations of other personages. Yet the State Assembly unanimously countenanced the proscription.

The Bharatiya Janata Party-led Gujarat government also banned Jaswant Singh's *Jinnah: India-Partition-Independence* in 2009, although it was overruled by the Gujarat High Court a few months later. Evidently, the ban was the result of intra-BJP politics. What the episode underlined was the fact that the sentiments and interests of politicians are more important than the rule of law. *Nine Hours To Rama* (1962), a novel by Stanley Wolpert, was also banned for similar reasons. Subjecting the people responsible for the security lapses that led to Gandhi's assassination as well as the assassin's political background and mental state to close scrutiny, it was also depicted on celluloid in Hollywood; the movie was also banned. Obviously, what was threatened in this case was the reputation of some important people, certainly not national security, India's friendly relations with other countries, public order, decency, morality, *etc.* Nor was there anything reasonable in the ban of the book *Shivaji: Hindu King in Islamic India* by James Laine by the Maharashtra government. Ditto with Sunanda Datta-Ray's *Smash and Grab: Annexation of Sikkim* which was banned in 1984. Bertrand Russell's *Unarmed Victory* was proscribed in 1963, for it showed our political masters during the India-China war in poor light. There was no rationale behind the bans imposed on these and other books.

Propensity to ban

Cinema, owing to its mass appeal, has suffered more than literature in terms of proscription. Chauvinism could be leftwing as well as rightwing in India when it comes to action against creative freedom. It is clear that when sentiments rule public discourse, reason is crucified; and the restrictions, which are supposed to be reasonable, actually pave the path for sentimental perversions and petty politicking.

Chapter 10

Hurting the sentiments-II

The Offence Principle (See Chapter I) sounds innocuous but has the potential of becoming a dangerous tool in the hands of the people inimical to not just the freedom of expression but all civil liberties an individual enjoys, or is supposed to enjoy, in a democracy. This principle can wreak havoc on anything said or written; let alone the opinions of common people, it can be used to carry out a tirade against the greatest creations of the human mind.

It may appear bizarre but no great book has been written which cannot be accused of offending some tetchy group or, in the Indian context, 'hurting the sentiments' of somebody or the other. From religious texts to philosophical and literary classics to pulp fiction, all of them have portions which would be found unpalatable from the perspective of the twenty-first century, and surely violate the dogmas of political correctness.

Politically incorrect philosophers

For Plato, slavery was a natural state of affairs, something which never bothered the great philosopher. His disciple and another great thinker, Aristotle, actually justified slavery. According to him:

> But is there any one thus intended by nature to be a slave, and for whom such a condition is expedient and right, or rather is

> not all slavery a violation of nature? There is no difficulty in answering this question, on grounds both of reason and of fact. For that some should rule and others be ruled is a thing not only necessary, but expedient; from the hour of their birth, some are marked out for subjection, others for rule.

Nor did the two gents (and many other thinkers) have very nice things to say about women. This, however, does not mean that Plato and Aristotle were not among the greatest philosophers of all time. In fact, A.N. Whitehead, the English mathematician and philosopher (1861-1947) went on to say that the safest general characterisation of the European philosophical tradition is that it consists of a series of footnotes to Plato. That may be an exaggeration but the importance and influence of the Greek duo could scarcely be over emphasised. Yet, the views of Plato and Aristotle make them good targets for a ban or abridgement of their works.

Then there was the *enfant terrible* of Western philosophy, Nietzsche. Here are some of his gems: 'Thou goest to woman? Do not forget thy whip!' 'Man should be educated for war, and woman for the recreation of the warrior; all else is folly.' 'Let woman be a plaything.' 'Everything about woman has one solution: pregnancy.' Another great German philosopher, Schopenhauer, whom Nietzsche considered as his teacher, did not make many edifying comments about the fair sex:

> It is only a man whose intellect is clouded by his sexual impulse that could give the name of the *fair sex* to that under-sized, narrow-shouldered, broad-hipped, and short-legged race, for the whole beauty of the sex is bound up with this impulse. Instead of calling them beautiful, there would be more warrant for describing women as the unaesthetic sex. Neither for music, nor for poetry, nor for the fine arts, have they really and truly any sense of susceptibility; it is a mere mockery if they make a pretense of it in order to assist their endeavor to please... They are incapable of taking a purely objective interest in anything... The most distinguished intellects among the whole sex have never managed to produce a single achievement in the fine arts that is really genuine and original; or given to the world any work of permanent value in any sphere.

The Indian scene

In India too, great authors have expressed uncharitable views about women. Tulsidas famously said that they, along with others, were fit to be beaten at will. '*Dhol Ganvar Shudra Pashu Naari, sakal tadna ke adhikari*,' the great saint poet wrote. This roughly translates as 'Illiterate bumpkins, beasts, lower caste people, and women ought to be beaten.' The list of great authors who have said politically incorrect things about women is long. If we accept that anything that offends some people should be banned or edited, these philosophers and thinkers would face censorship.

It is not just the views expressed by philosophers that would suffer vicious attacks. All classics, Indian as well as Western, can be targeted for promoting improper ideas or thoughts. And we are not even discussing *Lady Chatterley's Lover* and *Ulysses*, classics which did face charges of obscenity even in the West. *Madame Bovary* and *Anna Karenina* could also be accused of glamorising, if not promoting, adultery. *Gone with the Wind* is open to the criticism that it portrays slavery as practised in the American South in soft focus. Dante's *Divine Comedy* depicts the Prophet Mohammad in a bad light.

Indian literary works can face charges of exalting ideals and values that would harm any society. Agyey's *Shekhar: Ek jiwani* has shades of an incestuous relationship. Premchand's *Nirmala* also has a similar implication. Bimal Mitra's *Sahib Bibi aur Ghulam*, on which a great Hindi film was also made, is all about the decadence of feudalism, complete with mentions of debauchery and profligacy. U.R. Anantha Murthy's Kannada novel, *Samskara*, exposes the hollowness of Hindu traditions. Bankim Chandra's *Anandmath* does not have a very charitable mention of Muslims.

The point that I want to make is that if offending the sensibilities or hurting the sentiments is accepted as a parameter for proscribing or limiting a creative work, it will be a serious setback to the freedom of expression, for practically every great work will satisfy this parameter. Whipping up frenzy among the people and transmogrifying them into a rabble, any political party, pressure group, or publicity-seeker can build up a campaign against any book of philosophy, history, or literature. They do that quite often, at least in India.

Thankfully, there is extensive freedom in book writing and academia. But when it comes to the mass media, the considerations of political correctness and the tetchiness of troublemakers have to be taken into account.

History as morality play

This is the reason that we don't have many movies with a historical setting. A couple of points need to be made in this context. First, Hindus tend to see history as a morality play. In their scheme of things, Tipu Sultan was good because he fought the bad British, the fanatical streak in his personality notwithstanding. The Marathas were good because they fought the British. The good Gandhi fought the bad British. The result, however, was both good (Independence) and bad (Partition).

Second, the Hindus, being idolaters, worship anybody who they think has done good for the country, be it Subhash Chandra Bose or Sachin Tendulkar. I remember an incident of typical Indian idolatry. In January 2006, playing in Lahore, Rahul Dravid and Virendra Sehwag missed breaking the first-wicket partnership record by just four runs. The fifty-year-old record of Vinoo Mankad and Pankaj Roy of 413 runs remained intact. Sehwag's remark that he had never heard of Mankad occasioned indignation. The reaction of a prominent cricket writer and historian was extreme. Speaking on a television channel, he condemned Sehwag in the strongest terms for his ignorance of a cricketing legend from India. The historian's point was that Sehwag should respect, if not worship, Mankad. Sehwag's double century was overshadowed by his ignorance—as if he were a cricket historian and not a cricketer! This can happen only in a society which places authority and convention above endeavour and accomplishment.

This is also a typical Indian response to our past. We should give due deference to, if not venerate, historical personages. They ought to be shown with a halo, like Richard Attenborough's hagiographical *Gandhi*. We consider historical figures as gods and devils, angels and demons, not as human beings. Unsurprisingly, not many filmmakers dare to touch historical subjects.

Ketan Mehta is among the few who did. In August 2005, his *Mangal Pandey: The Rising* was released. Based on the life of Mangal Pandey, it was the story of the 1857 Revolt, also called by nationalists as 'India's First War of Independence.' Aamir Khan played the protagonist in the film. The principal Opposition party, the Bhartiya Janata Party, wanted the movie banned. It alleged that a hero of Indian history, Mangal Pandey, had been maligned. The party took offence at the depiction of Pandey visiting a brothel. In the Rajya Sabha, Samajwadi Party leader Uday Pratap Singh, also demanded a ban on the movie for the 'inaccurate portrayal' of Pandey. The Uttar Pradesh government also slammed the film for the 'distortion' of historical facts. There were protests, some of them violent, in the Hindi heartland where Pandey belonged.

Three years later, Ashutosh Gowariker's *Jodhaa Akbar* also ran into trouble with some Rajput groups. The sixteenth century love story about the Mughal Emperor Akbar and the Rajput Princess Jodhaa faced problems from many quarters. Apart from the Rajput groups, some historians also claimed Jodhaa was not Akbar's but his son Jehangir's wife. An apology was sought from Gowariker. It was the Supreme Court that came to the rescue of the filmmaker.

The objections may have nothing to do with any scholarly debate; any cantankerous person can trouble any filmmaker. As mentioned earlier, the objection to the movie titled *Billu Barber*, for instance, was ludicrous. These are, however, some of the most prominent instances of the Offence Principle going overboard in our country. Unfortunately, the state and people of India have tacitly accepted this principle; it is implemented so that the sentiments of any person or group are not hurt, much to the detriment of liberty.

Chapter 11

Freedom and science are inseparable

Is there any relationship between individual liberty and science? Empirical evidence suggests a very strong correlation between the two. Most Nobel Prizes in Science have been won by people from Western countries with the United States leading the list. And that's for real. I haven't come across any instance of an Indian, Pakistani, Chinese, or Arab scientist being discriminated so that a Westerner could get the coveted prize.

It says something about the intellectual and cultural ecosystem of India that not a single Indian *citizen* has won a Nobel for Science after Independence. A few Indians did win the award, but they had ceased to be the citizens of India when they did that. Har Gobind Khorana (1922-2011) shared the 1968 Nobel Prize for Physiology or Medicine with two other scientists for research in genetics. Similarly, Subrahmanyan Chandrasekhar (1910-95) was awarded the 1983 Nobel Prize for Physics, along with another scientists for fundamental discoveries in astrophysics. In 2009 Venkatraman Ramakrishnan (1952), along with two other scienties, won the Nobel Prize in Chemistry for studies of the structure and function of the ribosome.

The only Indian citizen to have won a Nobel Science was C.V. Raman(1888-1970) for the discovery that, while traversing a transparent material, some of the light that is deflected changes in wavelength. This has been named the Raman effect. But he won it in 1830, that is, before Independence.

The point I am trying to make is that there is a deep relationship between freedom and science. I would like to quote from Professor Judea Pearl's speech on the subject. Born in 1936, he is a computer scientist and philosopher, whose work in the probabilistic approach to artificial intelligence is well known. He is also the father of journalist Daniel Pearl, who was kidnapped and murdered by jihadists in Pakistan in 2002.

The course of truth

On 21 June 2007, Professor Pearl received an Honorary Doctorate in Science from the University of Toronto. At the convocation ceremony, Professor Pearl spoke on 'Science and Human Freedom.' He said:

> Galileo always reminds me of the inextricable connection between science and freedom... How? Because Galileo showed that to be a scientist you must have both respect for the truth and the audacity to believe that you can find it. This might sound trivial. Science, by definition, is about truth, so what's all this talk about freedom?
>
> It is not so trivial. Truth can be elusive, even in our times, covered by the heavy fog of fear and hidden agenda. It is only after the murder of my son Danny that I came to appreciate how hard it is, even in the age of internet, to stay the course of truth.
>
> ...What Galileo showed us is that you cannot have one honesty without the other; scientific truth demands scientific honesty and scientific honesty demands intellectual honesty overall.
>
> We all remember the 1,000 years of zero scientific progress through the Middle Ages. What caused it?
>
> The conventional answer is that the Church was repressive of scientific discourse. But this could not be the whole story. There was no repressive Church in the Muslim world. And Muslim scientists had access to the richest libraries of the time, well-funded astronomical observatories and all the writings of the Greek and Roman philosophers. So why didn't a genius like

Galileo emerge in Cordoba or Alexandria or Baghdad in the Eighth or Ninth century?

Why was science held back, in almost total stagnation for 1,000 years, until, as though by miracle, the genius of Copernicus, Vieta, and Galileo emerged in the Dark Ages of Europe, of all places? Can you imagine where mankind would be today had the Renaissance and the Scientific Revolution taken place in the Fifth century instead of the Fifteenth?

What Galileo taught us is that the permission to read, translate, observe, and use fancy equipment is not enough; the development of science requires a restless and rebellious spirit, a spirit that puts the individual at the center of the universe and proclaims: 'I don't care about Aristotle and his fancy books, I want to see these two rocks dropped from the tower of Pisa and I want to see them with my own two eyes.'

In other words, what Galileo showed us is that you cannot truly search for the truth unless you are free to rebel against the detractors of truth: conventional wisdom, peer pressure, sacred cows, wishful thinking, revered authority and hidden agenda, in short, free to perceive yourself as an *agent*, in control of your destiny, not an *object*, at the mercy of destiny.

Remarkably, this Western perception of man as a free agent, sometimes called the 'scientific philosophy', is not always taken for granted, even today.

Professor Pearl quoted Sheik Yusuf Qaradawi in his speech. In his address to Al Jazeera listeners, Qaradawi once said: 'Take from the West all its science and technology, but you must reject Western philosophy, because it is corrupt at its roots by the pagan philosophies of Greece and Rome.' Professor Pearl responded to this statement, saying, 'Sorry to disappoint you, Sheik Yusuf Qaradawi, but you can't have science and technology without Western philosophy of freedom, honesty, and individual *agency*; it has been tried before, for 1,000 years, in your own courtyard, and failed.'

Science and technology are part of the package that the Western civilisation offers, and the package is a seamless whole whose one element cannot be extracted without disturbing everything else. This is the reason that no Indian *national* has won a Nobel Prize in Science after Independence, though several persons of Indian origin have done that. This is not surprising, because India does not offer the ecosystem in which liberty can grow. Similarly, Arab and Muslim nations have not done any wonders in the realm of science; even petrodollars have created ritzy malls, fantastic engineering feats—using mainly Western skills—but have not triggered indigenous science and technology. A viewpoint similar to Qaradawi's was expressed by Swami Vivekananda in a lecture in 1898. He said:

> Why are we so backwards nowadays? ... If we want to rise, we must also remember that we have many things to learn from the West. We should learn from the West her arts and her sciences. From the West we have to learn the sciences of physical nature, while on the other hand the West has to come to us to learn and assimilate religion and spiritual knowledge. We Hindus must believe that we are the teachers of the world... So, I must call upon you to go out to England and America, not as beggars but as teachers of religion.

In short, while the West is superior in natural sciences and material aspects, it has to learn from India in matters related to the spiritual. Vivekananda was unarguably the pioneer in nurturing, if not creating, the myth that the West is inferior to India in religious and spiritual aspects. It was a shrewd ploy: while the admission of Indian weakness was verifiable (the West was obviously much ahead of us in material aspects), the claim of superior Indian spiritualism was not. The myth perfectly suited the nationalistic mood of the time.

Over a century later, we must drop this notion. There is nothing in contemporary India to suggest that 'the West has to come to us to learn and assimilate religion and spiritual knowledge.'

Religion as intoxicant

One of the most quoted of Karl Marx's statements is: 'It [religion] is the opium of the people.' When he wrote this in 1843, opium was an important medicine. It was used as a painkiller, palliative, or sedative as also a cure for number of diseases, including cholera. The use of opium soothes nerves, makes one introverted, gives hallucinations, and generally makes the user quiet and calm. In India however, religion is like an alcoholic intoxicant. Unlike opium, alcohol excites nerves, makes one extroverted and talkative, gives a sense of false power, and is likely to make the user violent and unruly. This can be observed with the Kanwarias, whose annual pilgrimage to the Himalayas has become a nuisance for people using the same route; including the Sikh youth, who have been indulging in hooliganism and stunts on the roads of Connaught Place in the Capital on weekends, after paying obeisance at Bangla Sahib;and also the Muslim youth who indulge in similar stunts on roads. Muslim youth also perform stunts on Shab-e-Barat, the blessed night. This is frowned upon by clerics. *The Times of India* (22 May2016) quoted Maulana Mateen-ul-Haq Usama Qasmi of Kanpur: 'Such revelry is forbidden on a night when Prophet Muhammad is believed to have visited a graveyard and prayed for the departed souls. Those indulging in unlawful activities like stunts on motorcycles will incur Allah's wrath.' He also exhorted parents to monitor the activities of their children.

When Indians go to temples and gurdwaras, organise religious functions, or go on pilgrimage, often piety is mixed with pretension; it is not just the ennobling features of the faith that move them; frequently, a desire to flaunt religiosity is more prominent. Religion in India has become an intoxicant, which gives the faithful a high that few spirits can match. The fact that no stigma is associated with such intoxication emboldens the faithful a great deal. So, it is advisable to steer clear of Kanwarias and Muslim and Sikh bikers.

Vivekananda was grossly wrong: we have to learn the arts and sciences from the West but, equally if not more importantly, also imbibe its philosophic and intellectual tradition. Science and technology has failed to take off not only in the Muslim world but also in India, a country which boasts of not only an ancient civilisation but many original contributions to science and technology, and rigorous and profound systems of philosophy.

Science in ancient India

Let us list a few achievements of Indians in science and technology.

I rely on the authority of A.L. Basham regarding the achievements of Indians in science and technology. In *The Wonder That Was India: A Survey of the Culture of the Indian Sub-Continent Before the Coming of the Muslims*, he wrote:

> the learned realised, perhaps through the influence of Greek astronomy, that it [the shape of earth] was in fact spherical. Various estimates of its size were made, the most popularising

> that of Brahmagupta (seventh century A.D.), who gave its circumference as 5,000 *yojanas*. Assuming Brahmagupta's *yojana* to be the short league of about 4.5 miles, this figure is not far out, and is as accurate as any given by ancient astronomers.

Aryabhata even proposed a heliocentric theory, as Basham pointed out:

> For purposes of calculation the planetary system was taken as geocentric, though Aryabhata in the fifth century suggested that the earth revolved round the sun and rotated on its axis; this theory was also known to later astronomers, but it never affected astronomical practice. The precession of the equinoxes was known, and calculated with some accuracy by medieval astronomers, as were the lengths of the year, the lunar month, and other astronomical constants. These calculations were reliable for most practical purposes, and in many cases more exact than those of the Greco-Roman world. Eclipses were forecast with accuracy and their true cause understood.

Basham also highlighted Indians' contribution to mathematics:

> The success of Indian mathematics was mainly due to the fact that the Indians had a dear conception of abstract number, as distinct from numerical quantity of objects or spatial extension. While Greek mathematical science was largely based on mensuration and geometry, India transcended these conceptions quite early, and, with the aid of a simple numeral notation, devised a rudimentary algebra which allowed more complicated calculations than were possible to the Greeks, and led to the study of number for its own sake.

In other words, a fundamental flaw of the Indian intellectual tradition—more emphasis on abstruseness than on real-life situations—had a serendipitous effect in mathematics, the most abstract of sciences.: 'The earliest inscription recording the date by a system of nine digits and a zero, with place notation for the tens and hundreds, comes from Gujarat, and is dated A.D. 595,' he added.

There was indeed a tradition of mathematics:

> Medieval Indian mathematicians, such as Brahmagupta (seventh century), Mahavir (ninth century) and Bhaskara (twelfth century), made several discoveries which in Europe were not known until the Renaissance or later. They understood the import of positive and negative quantities, evolved sound systems of extracting square and cube roots, and could solve quadratic and certain types of indeterminate equations. For pi Aryabhata gave the usual modern approximate value of 3.1416... This value of pi, much more accurate than that of the Greeks, was improved to nine places of decimals by later Indian mathematicians. Some steps were made in trigonometry, spherical geometry and calculus, chiefly in connection with astronomy. The mathematical implications of zero (sunya) and infinity, never more than vaguely realized by classical authorities, were fully understood in medieval India...[Bhaskara]... established mathematically what had been recognized in Indian theology at least a millennium earlier, that infinity, however divided, remains infinite...

Basham went on to add:

> Most of the great discoveries and inventions of which Europe is so proud would have been impossible without a developed system of mathematics, and this in turn would have been impossible if Europe had been shackled by the unwieldy system of Roman numerals. The unknown man who devised the new system was from the world's point of view, after the Buddha, the most important son of India. His achievement, though easily taken for granted, was the work of an analytical mind of the first order, and he deserves much more honour than he has so far received.

There were also interesting developments in medical science:

> Ancient Indian doctors had no clear knowledge of the function of the brain, and believed with many ancient peoples that the

> heart was the seat of intelligence. They realized, however, the importance of the spinal cord, and knew of the existence of the nervous system, though it was not properly understood... Despite their inaccurate knowledge of physiology, which was by no means inferior to that of most ancient peoples, India evolved a developed empirical surgery. The caesarian section was known, bone-setting reached a high degree of skill, and plastic surgery was developed far beyond anything known elsewhere at the time. Ancient Indian surgeons were expert at the repair of noses, ears and lips, lost or injured in battle or by judicial mutilation. In this respect Indian surgery remained ahead of European until the 18th century, when the surgeons of the East Indian Company were not ashamed to learn the art of rhinoplasty from the Indians.

In short, there was a strong, healthy tradition of science in India, and there are various achievements Indians can be proud of, but it is evident that many claims made by nationalists, including Prime Minister Narendra Modi, are wild exaggerations.

Further, science somehow disappeared from India in the second millennium. Why and how did it happen?

What Orientals lacked

Indians did not lack scientific spirit or intellectual rigour, as is evident from the remarkable progress made in so many fields. Yet, two things were missing. One was the osmotic relationship between philosophy and the various sciences and arts. Great Indian philosophers rarely came out of their ivory towers; they revelled in their theological flights, ignoring the hard realities, overlooking the findings of sciences and thus, denying their philosophies the enlivening inputs. It is because of their isolation from the real world that for centuries, and ignorance of scientific development, they persisted with the same examples like the snake-rope illusion and the colour of the conch.

The second thing that was missing in our intellectual tradition was the emphasis on the individual, in contradistinction to such metaphysical concepts as *atma* and *brahman* (soul and ultimate reality) of the orthodox schools of Indian philosophy. The free individual *agent* was missing.

The Chinese, too, made remarkable progress in science and technology; indeed, the world is indebted to them for many inventions such as the press and compass which greatly influenced the course of history. English philosopher Francis Bacon wrote in *Novum Organum*:

> Printing, gunpowder and the compass: These three have changed the whole face and state of things throughout the world; the first in literature, the second in warfare, the third in navigation; whence have followed innumerable changes, in so much that no empire, no sect, no star seems to have exerted greater power and influence in human affairs than these mechanical discoveries.

Yet, as in India, science in China did not have much of an osmotic relationship between philosophy and science and between science and the political-economic system. As Professor Pearl said:

> ...you cannot truly search for the truth unless you are free to rebel against the detractors of truth: conventional wisdom, peer pressure, sacred cows, wishful thinking, revered authority and revered authority and hidden agenda, in short, free to perceive yourself as an agent, in control of your destiny, not an object, at the mercy of destiny.

In other words, science without freedom is austere instrumentalism; scientific achievements are discrete developments unrelated to each other and unconnected with the *weltanschauung*. Unsurprisingly, every Oriental *weltanschauung* is underpinned with esoteric metaphysics, and worse, religion and spirituality. India and China did have scientific development but no Scientific Revolution, Renaissance, Enlightenment, or the Age of Reason. The two Asian giants—indeed the entire Orient—still await them.

Chapter 12

Freedom and faith

Religion is one of the most important subjects that are discussed, debated, and analysed all over the world. Some of the profoundest thinkers have contemplated and written about it. Yet, there is no general agreement, or even broad consensus, on the nature of religion.

There are almost as many definitions of religion as there are philosophers of religion. According to the famous American pragmatist thinker, William James, it is the 'belief that there is an unseen order and that our supreme good lies in harmoniously adjusting ourselves thereto.' For the British philosopher, Alfred North Whitehead, religion is 'what the individual does with his own solitariness.' George Hegel found religion as 'the knowledge possessed by the finite mind of its nature as absolute mind.' Then there is Matthew Arnold: 'the true meaning of religion is thus, not simply morality, but morality touched by emotion.' Religious faith, said the existentialist theologian Paul Tillich, 'is the state of being ultimately concerned.' For the atheistic Karl Marx, 'Religion is the sigh of the oppressed creature, the heart of a heartless world and the soul of soulless conditions. It is the opium of the people.'

In *The Golden Bough*, James Fraser writes that 'religion consists of two elements, a theoretical and a practical, namely, a belief in powers higher than man and an attempt to propitiate or please them. Of the two, belief clearly comes first, since we must believe in the existence of a divine being before we can attempt to please him. But unless the belief leads to a corresponding practice, it is not a religion but merely a theology...On the other hand, mere practice, divested of all religious belief, is also not religion.'

John Hick, in his authoritative *Philosophy of Religion*, has quite appropriately defined religion, by using Wittgenstein's concept of 'language games', in terms of 'family resemblances.' According to Hick:

> In much religion there is the worship of a God or gods; but in Theravada Buddhism, for example, there is not. Again, religion often makes for social cohesion; yet in some strands it is aptly characterised as 'what man does with his solitariness' (A.N. Whitehead). Again, religion often makes for the inner harmony of the individual; yet some of the greatest religious innovators seemed to their contemporaries to be unbalanced and even insane. The family resemblances model allows for such differences…
>
> Within the ramifying set of family resemblances there is, however, one feature which is extremely widespread even though not universal. This is a concern with what is variously called salvation or liberation… All the greatly developed world faiths… offer a transition from a radically unsatisfactory state to a limitlessly better one.

The great thinkers have been right on various aspects of religion. It indeed, as William James says, involves a belief in transcendentalism. Similarly, there cannot be religion without solitude or without a feeling of being a part of something grander than human conception. Ethics too are either derived from or are a function of some sort of religious beliefs. Tillich's definition of faith as 'the state of being ultimately concerned' is also not inaccurate. As Hick explained, it is not only the concern which is ultimate—in the sense that there is no concern greater than faith—but also the state. Marx, despite his antipathy towards things religious and metaphysical, is right in seeing religion as the 'opium of the people.' Hick's description of religion, emphasising resemblances, is also quite appropriate.

However, all these definitions and expositions miss something. For instance, religion is not just the opium of the people but also their intoxicant, especially in India. Yes, being 'the sigh of the oppressed creature, 'religion calms the frayed nerves of the tortured human being. Even the most fatalistic of religions prepares man intellectually, spiritually, and axiologically, to face the slings and arrows of outrageous fortune. However, if religion can be a sedative, it can also be firewater.

We intend to define religion in a manner that is complete and comprehensive. We define it as transcendental rationalisation which permeates *modus vivendi*. It profoundly influences man's life by shaping his worldview and belief in transcendental principles, moulding his morals and manners, and fashioning his behavior. This also includes an important aspect of religion which is implicit in its etymology. About the origin and etymology of religion, Merriam-Webster says: 'Middle English religioun, from Anglo-French religiun, Latin religion-, religio supernatural constraint, sanction, religious practice, perhaps from religare to restrain, tie back.' Similarly, the Sanskrit word 'dharma', when translated as 'religion', means something that ought to be upheld. Our definition includes both these terms as well.

Weltanschauung in action

We assert that religion is the human response to the world—the world man lives in, the world as he comprehends it, the everyday world; it is also a response to the world that is often beyond the ken of rational comprehension. Religion is human response to the intelligible and the ineffable, to the finite and the infinite. It is traditional *weltanschauung* in action.

Religion gives meaning to the world—at any rate, for most people—which otherwise seems so full of contradictions and unjustness; often, it gives a meaning to our lives. In the ultimate analysis, religion is rationalisation par excellence. It explains the myriad injustices, contradictions, incongruities, paradoxes, and absurdities man faces on earth. Why are there wars, earthquakes, floods, famines, and other calamities claiming so many innocent lives? Why are so many young lives cut short in accidents and crimes, whereas almost all politicians live long? Why do so many good people suffer? Why do scoundrels flourish? Why do so many suffer from so many diseases? Why are some people born with congenital diseases? There is a large number of such questions which no philosopher or philosophy has been able to answer convincingly. Religion answers these questions.

The answers may not be logically tenable or philosophically sound; but then ordinary people do not seek recondite syllogisms that impress logicians; people seek explanations that are simple as well as all-encompassing. Religion mostly relies on—what logical positivist philosopher A.J. Ayer called—'unverifiable' principles and entities, the theory of karma and the concept Christian God being two examples.

Our festivals and carnivals, celebrations and mourning, customs and rituals spring from our religious beliefs, moulding the *modus vivendi* into the grammar of faith. Religious communities come into being. The etymological aspects can scarcely be over emphasised in such developments. By creating bonds of faith and upholding beliefs common to the community, religion instills a sense of bonding among the faithful. This creates a religious identity which goes on to define not only the social and cultural aspects but sometimes even the political and economic facets of the people.

Life beyond hunger

Religion is also a higher calling for a large number of people. Man does not live by bread alone, Jesus said. Man also yearns to go beyond his immediate needs. Hence the arts, literature, music, culture. And hence religion. In pre-modern times, man's innate yearning for the infinite usually had only one channel—religious. So, most of art and culture, both in the East and the West, was animated by religious themes and motifs.

It is primarily in modern times that the finer aspects of human life became secular in nature. For industrialisation, the economic system of modern society exponentially augments production, creates huge wealth-generation possibilities, and increases prosperity, thus giving people considerable amount of time and resources to indulge in pursuits other than breadwinning.

A big difference between the West and India is that while industrialisation brought enormous changes in social mores, intellectual pursuits, cultural activities, political ethos, and religious practices in the former, our country was not able to fully come to terms with the imperatives of modernity. We have had considerable modernisation but little modernity. A comparative study of modernisation in India and the West is beyond the scope of this book, but three points need to be made in our context.

First, philistinism being rampant in India, not many people like to read books or pursue the finer aspects of life. According to a couplet by the Sanskrit classical poet Bharthahari, those who are without literature, music, and fine arts are actually beasts without tails and horns. In short, refinement is the defining feature of human existence. Sadly, it is lacking in our country. In North India in particular, it is rare to find a bookshelf in the houses of reasonably well-off people. People spend many lakhs of rupees on electronic gadgetry, bathroom fittings, car accessories, and trivia, but when it comes to books, they would prefer to borrow them from somebody. Arts, music, theatre—it is almost the same story everywhere. Most people drown themselves in the shallowness of pulp fiction, mediocre cinema, television shows, the faster forms of cricket, and other mediums of recreation—the forms that offer transient pleasure but not deeply felt joy, the modes of entertainment that excite the senses without caressing the heart and soul, the pastimes that fail to bridge or even shorten the distance between the self and the infinite. The crude and the crass rule the roost. The core of the persona remains hollow.

When a man, therefore, faces a life-defining moment—an unexpected death, some tragedy, some startling or unsettling development—he has few inner reserves to draw energies from. More often than not, religion comes to his rescue as 'the sigh of the oppressed creature, the heart of a heartless world, and the soul of soulless conditions.' It is, then, nescience and the benighted state rather than profundity that nudges people towards religion.

This brings us to the second point: the renowned religiosity in India lacks a solid philosophical core. Indians proudly claim that the philosophical tradition in their country is thousands of years old, that there have been many schools of thinking, that many theories and concepts of modern Western philosophers were anticipated by Hindu sages, and so on.

Past glories, however, should not be used to overlook the pathetic state of cultural, spiritual, and religious life in India. Contemporary Hinduism has been reduced to elaborate rituals, ever-proliferating pilgrimages and sects, and ostentatious religiosity. It has little to do with the ennobling of being, the quest of the infinite or 'an unseen order,' one's romance with one's solitariness, blending morality with emotion, or being 'ultimately concerned.'

The third and final point worth emphasising is that without freedom of expression, it is impossible to get out of the morass of rituals and rites. In fact, more than science it is religion that needs liberty. A Galileo is persecuted, but a Jesus is crucified. Great religious leaders, from the Buddha, Mahavir, and Jesus to Nanak, Kabir, Martin Luther, and Swami Dayanand Saraswati of Arya Samaj could not have expounded their principles had they not used this freedom. Nor could any religious personage or profound thinker propound anything remarkable if he is worried about the sentiments of all publicity seekers, the equations of political parties, the tetchiness of the sanctimonious, and so on. In short, religion without freedom of expression is pure entropy, the permanent locus of ritualism for the entire mankind.

Chapter 13

Script for political correctness

In Western countries, Right-leaning authors, columnists, and commentators often bemoan the cantankerousness and absurdities of political correctness. This is not surprising because Political Correctness (PC) has become not only an abomination plaguing common parlance and free speech but also a device for the Left to promote its irrationalities. In India, the situation is even worse; it is not just the Left, but practically all political parties and social organisations that ardently, and sometimes violently, champion some or other form of PC. At any rate, the casualty is always freedom of expression.

It is rare that violent PC is successfully checked. One such occasion was on 28 April 2010, when the Supreme Court came to the rescue of south Indian film actress Khushboo for her statement on pre-marital sex, virginity and live-in relationships. In an interview in 2005, she had said it was not wrong for women to have pre-marital sex as long as they took precautions. Further, the Tamil actress said, it was 'not fair of any educated youth to expect his wife to be a virgin.' She also found nothing objectionable in live-in relationships.

The reaction to her remarks was swift and severe. Many political parties and a few people from the film industry castigated her for, what they called, an attack on 'Tamil culture and values.' The Dalit Panthers of India (DPI) and another political party, the Pattali Makkal Katchi (PMK), protested against her; the protest often degenerated into violence.

But it was not the violent protestors and their instigators who were found to be on the wrong side of the law; Khushboo, on the other hand, faced more than twenty criminal suits filed against her. One reason was that the PMK was part of the ruling coalition in New Delhi, with its leader A. Ramadoss being the Union Health Minister at that time.

Hounded and mobbed

Hounded by the law and mobbed by the lawless, Khushboo offered an open apology to Tamils, especially women, saying she would never even dream of sullying the image of the Tamil people. 'Even in films, I never undertook roles that lowered the image of women,' she said in a statement. 'I have the greatest regard for Tamils, especially Tamil women. If my remarks have hurt anybody's feelings, I tender an apology. I am one among you and will always remain with you.' But her tormentors were unrelenting.

Relief for Khushboo came after years of prosecution, persecution, and vilification. It is interesting to note that the outfits which waged a jihad against her could scarcely be categorised as rightwing. The DPI claims to be fighting for the Dalits—literally, 'the oppressed.' These out castes were discriminated against in Hindu scriptures. The very name of the party was inspired by that of Black Panther Party of the US. The PMK too claims to represent a supposedly 'backward' community.

This brings us to another conspicuous feature of Indian politics: the proclivity of politicians to appeal to the crudest, crassest, and basest of public sentiments. The lyrics of a Hindi film song had to be changed; *Teli ka tel* (edible oil made by oil-maker) is replaced by *Dilli ka tel* (oil from Delhi) because the traditional oil-makers, or Telis, objected to the word. The mere mention of a word denoting a profession becomes politically incorrect.

Pandering to the lowest common denominator has put sanctimoniousness at a premium and has made reason a useless virtue—in fact, an avoidable vice. It has also ensured that PC in India fashions a trajectory for itself quite different from that in the West. Spewing gross sentimentalism brings immediate publicity which, in turn, sometimes also translates into political and pecuniary gains. Unsurprisingly, most attacks on the freedom of expression are made on the pretext that the movie, book, *etc.*, 'hurt the sentiments' of this or that community.

In this milieu, neo-puritanism of various kinds has gained currency. The totalitarian imperative is the thread that runs common to all puritanical thought. Be it the sanctimoniousness of radical Tamil outfits, Ramadoss' tirade against smoking on screen, or Hindu groups' crusade against Valentine's Day, at the root of the issue is the neo-puritans' belief that their worldview is incontrovertible, unimpeachable, and sacrosanct; thus, it is not only their right but also duty to impose their views on others. For they know the Truth, the Good, and the Beautiful; and as the custodians of wisdom, they ought to spread the Word—with force, if needed.

Smoking out freedom

Ramadoss' tirade against smoking on screen should be seen in this background. In 2005, he endeavoured to ban smoking in cinema and on television. The measure was opposed not only by filmmakers and other creative people but also by the Ministry of Information &Broadcasting. Officials of the ministry also raised questions about the implementation of the proposed ban. Their argument was that it was extremely difficult to depict characters that are traditionally linked with smoking. For instance, how could you show Churchill without his trademark cigar?

The Minister of Information & Broadcasting S. Jaipal Reddy said: 'We have already sought exemptions on a large number of serials, films, treatment of historical characters and literature and classics.' The Central Board of Film Certification also did not like Ramadoss' idea.

As is the wont of the politically correct, Ramadoss took recourse to *argumentum ad hominem*—imputing ulterior motives to the views expressed by his opponents rather than rationally responding to their arguments. On 22 September 2005, he was quoted in a newspaper saying that some officials in the Information and Broadcasting Ministry were part of the anti-ban lobby: 'I don't see any tussle with the Information and Broadcasting Ministry. The lobby is strong and even some of the Information and Broadcasting officials are part of this lobby. I am going to take it all the way.'

Threatening to impose the Cigarettes and Other Tobacco Products Act 2003, he said, 'Movie is an indirect advertisement. We are going to ban on-screen smoking under anti-tobacco Act which is under the health ministry. If anybody transgresses, we are going to take action under the anti-tobacco Act.' Quoting a study published in the journal *Lancet*, according to which fifty-two per cent of children take up smoking after watching it done in films, Ramadoss said, 'When children in the age of twelve, thirteen, fourteen start smoking because they see their heroes smoking, then it is my duty to stop them from smoking.'

While tobacco is dangerous and smoking in cinema does influence impressionable minds, these facts do not warrant a ban. There are other activities—like robbery, murder and rape—which are also shown in films. There is also evidence that many people get ideas from movies and commit crimes. Ultimately, everything boils down to individual responsibility. One can be influenced by anything—movies, television serials, newspaper reports; it is a matter of making a choice. The choice has to be made by the individual, not by the state or somebody claiming to be the custodian of wisdom.

Custodians of tradition

Some Hindu groups claim to be the custodians of tradition and wisdom. They campaign against the celebration of Valentine's Day which they assert, is alien, indeed inimical, to Indian culture. They attack shops selling Valentine Cards and related merchandise; often young couples are assaulted. Vandalism and violence are managed, orchestrated; even the media is invited to record the vehemence of the protestors. Rarely are the attackers punished by the law, or even checked effectively.

The enemies of pleasure and joy are also impelled by totalitarian beliefs. By the way, it needs to be mentioned here that it is not only radical Hindu outfits which are opposed to Valentine's Day. Thanks to rampant political correctness, the opposition of fundamentalist Islam and the Left to the celebration of love goes unnoticed in our country. Jamie Glazov, *Frontpage Magazine* editor, posted an article on 12 February2011.[7] He wrote:

> ... February 14, is Valentine's Day, the sacred day that intimate companions mark to celebrate their love and affection for one another. If you're thinking about making a study of how couples celebrate this day, the Muslim world and the milieus of the radical Left are not the places you should be spending most, if any, of your time. Indeed, it's pretty hard to outdo jihadists and 'progressives' when it comes to the hatred of Valentine's Day. And this hatred is precisely the territory on which the contemporary romance between the radical Left and Islamic fanaticism is formed.

7 See http://www.frontpagemag.com

The train is never late: every time Valentine's Day comes around, the Muslim world reacts with ferocious rage, with its leaders doing everything in their power to quash the festivity that comes with the celebration of private romance. Imams around the world thunder against Valentine's Day every year, and the celebration of the day itself is literally outlawed in Islamist states. The Saudis, for instance, ruthlessly punish the slightest hint of celebrating Valentine's Day. Just a few days ago, the Kingdom and its religious 'morality' police officially issued a stern warning that anyone caught even thinking about Valentine's Day will suffer some of the most painful penalties of Sharia law. This is typical of the Saudis, of course. As Daniel Pipes has reported, the Saudi regime takes a firm stand against Valentine's Day every year, and the Saudi religious police monitor stores selling roses and other gifts. They have even arrested women for wearing red on that day...

The Iranian despots, meanwhile, are trying to make sure the Saudis don't outdo them in suffocating Valentine's Day. Iran's 'morality' police order shops to remove heart-and-flower decorations and images of couples embracing on this day, and anytime around this day. In Pakistan, the student wing of the fundamentalist Islamic party Jamaat-e-Islami has called for a complete ban on Valentine's Day celebrations. Khalid Waqas Chamkani, a leader in the party, calls it a 'shameful day.'

Typical of this whole pathology in the Islamic world, was a development witnessed back on 10 February 2006, when activists of the radical Kashmiri Islamic group Dukhtaran-e-Millat (Daughters of the Community) went on a rampage in Srinagar, the main city of the Indian portion of Kashmir. Some two dozen black-veiled Muslim women stormed gift and stationery shops, burning Valentine's Day cards and posters showing couples together.

In the West, meanwhile leftist feminists are not to be outdone by their jihadi allies in reviling— and trying to kill— Valentine's

Day. Throughout all Women's Studies Programs on American campuses, for instance, one will find the demonisation of Valentine's Day, since, as the disciples of Andrea Dworkin angrily explain, 'the day is a manifestation of how capitalist and homophobic patriarchs brainwash and oppress women and push them into spheres of powerlessness…'

So what exactly is transpiring here? What explains this hatred of Valentine's Day by leftist feminists and jihadis? And how and why does it serve as the sacred bond that brings the radical Left and Islam into its current curve of solidarity?The core issue at the foundation of this phenomenon is that Islam and the radical Left both revile the notion of private love, a non-tangible and divine entity that draws individuals to each other and, therefore, distracts them from submitting themselves to a secular deity.

The highest objective of both Islam and the radical Left is clear: to shatter the sacred intimacy that a man and a woman can share with one another, for such a bond is inaccessible to the order. History, therefore, demonstrates how Islam, like Communism, wages a ferocious war on any kind of private and unregulated love. In the case of Islam, the reality is epitomised in its monstrous structures of gender apartheid and the terror that keeps it in place. Indeed, female sexuality and freedom are demonised and, therefore, forced veiling, forced marriage, female genital mutilation, honour killings and other misogynist monstrosities become mandatory parts of the sadistic paradigm…

Valentine's Day is a 'shameful day' for the Muslim world and for the radical Left. It is shameful because love is considered obscene, since it threatens the highest of values: the need for a totalitarian order to hold the complete and undivided attention, allegiance and veneration of every citizen. Love serves as the most lethal threat to the tyrants seeking to build Shariah and a classless Utopia on earth and so these tyrants yearn for the annihilation of every ingredient in man that smacks of anything human.

Whether it is an attack on Khushboo, onscreen smoking, or Valentine's Day, the idea is to impose totalitarianism of one kind or another. What is equally disturbing is the fact that the issue of freedom of expression gets diffused by the intellectual bankruptcy of opinion makers and the pusillanimity of those in power. When a Ramadoss begins an invective against onscreen smoking, objections are rarely raised about the curtailment of creative freedom; the debate meanders into irrelevance, sentimentalism, and trivia. Those who criticise or resist the proposal do it on pragmatic rather than principled grounds; they say that the implementation of a ban would be difficult; they don't say that the ban goes against the spirit of liberal democracy.

Paternalistic government

Even worse are certain traits in Indian society; people actually believe that the government should do everything to make their lives better, from improvingLaw & Order to eradicating poverty, reducing prices, promoting sports, and uplifting morals. I remember listening to an interactive radio programme on the issue of the ban on onscreen smoking; most people the anchor spoke to, supported Ramadoss' fanaticism. A country gets the rulers it deserves.

Similarly, in 2008 the Maharashtra Navnirman Sena (MNS) chief Raj Thackeray carried out a violent campaign against what he thought was an anti-Marathi remark made by reputed film star and the Samajwadi Party's Rajya Sabha MP Jaya Bachchan. At the music launch of the Hindi film *Drona*, she had said, '*Hum UP ke log hain, isliye Hindi mein baat karenge, Maharashtra ke log maaf kijiye*(We are from UP or Uttar Pradesh, so we will speak in Hindi. People of Maharashtra, please excuse us).'

Raj Thackeray condemned the comment for being against the people of Maharashtra. He sought an apology from her, failing which he threatened to ban all Bachchan films. MNS workers attacked the cinema halls screening *The Last Lear*, starringJaya Bachchan's husband Amitabh Bachchan. Amitabh Bachchan was forced to apologise. Raj pompously said: 'We accept Bachchan's apology and withdraw the boycott.' The MNS also withdrew the call to boycott his films.

Threats were made and carried out by Thackeray and his men; the administration remained a mute spectator for the ruling party, the Congress, was cozying up to him. Consider the perversity of the situation: the country's best-known acting couple is made to undergo trauma and humiliation in full public view because a parochial chieftain does not approve of certain remarks attributed to them. Their remarks and, for that matter, their movies do not violate any law of the land. Yet, they are persecuted and the persecutor also extracts an apology.

In a way, Raj Thackeray and several other people's terror tactics are aimed at preventing prominent personalities from expressing their views freely in a public forum; this leaves the public arena the preserve of professional politicians. This is not to say that the political class is conspiring to keep public figures out of politics, but waving the 'hurting-the-sentiments' flag does the job.

While Thackeray has his stormtroopers, other busybodies keep coming up with legal cases against creative works. In the 1980s, University of Denver professors Penelope Canan and George W. Pring coined a term, SLAPP, or Strategic Lawsuit Against Public Participation. This was a ploy to censor, intimidate, subdue and possibly silence anybody by imposing the cost and harassment of a legal defence.

In India, however, SLAPP is not always 'strategic'; it may be just some publicity-seeker or downright blackmailer who achieves his goals by legal means. The tragedy is that widespread political correctness provides a convenient backdrop to do that.

At the time of accepting the Bachchans' apology, a gloating Raj Thackeray said that from now on Jaya Bachchan should stick to the script and mouth 'only the dialogues written out for her.' Political correctness determines what our film stars and other public figures should say.

Chapter 14

Doublespeak by liberals

The doublespeak of India's liberals and Leftists on freedom of expression is as startling as it is disgraceful. When the Hindu groups indulge in vandalism, they cry themselves hoarse, quote John Stuart Mill, and demand that the rule of law be upheld. But when the culprits are Muslim fundamentalists, our intellectuals prefer to remain silent.

Consider the case of M.F. Husain's paintings about nude Hindu goddesses. In September 2008, the Supreme Court called his controversial painting 'Bharat Mata' a 'work of art.' The apex court's support for Husain was indeed a fillip to the cause of freedom in our country. The court's stand was intended to discourage testy people and publicity seekers who cry about 'hurt sentiments' and want to restrict the realm of creativity.

The petitioner's argument, that the depiction of a nude woman as Mother India hurt the sentiments of every sane citizen, did not cut any ice with the apex court bench, comprising Chief Justice K.G. Balakrishnan and Justices P. Sathasivam and J.M. Panchal. The bench asked: 'Does the sentiment of the petitioner get scandalised by the large number of photographs of erotic sculptures which are in circulation?' It explained that the sculptures like those of Khajuraho and Konark are not considered offensive; so, Husain's painting 'is an art like the sculptures. None gets scandalised looking at the sculptures.'

In May 2008, Justice Sanjay Kishan Kaul of the Delhi High Court had pronounced a similar verdict:

> It is very unfortunate that the works of any artist today who have tried to play around with nudity have come under scrutiny. They have to face the music, making them think twice before exhibiting their work. Criminal justice system should not be used as an easy recourse to ventilate against a creative art.

Court upholds freedom of expression

Justice Kaul indeed supported the freedom of expression:

> In real democracy the dissenter must feel at home and ought not to be nervously looking over his shoulder fearing captivity or bodily harm or economic and social sanctions for his unconventional or critical views. There should be freedom for the thought we hate. Freedom of speech has no meaning if there is no freedom after speech. The reality of democracy is to be measured by the extent of freedom and accommodation it extends.

He concluded the judgment on a high note, full of optimism: 'I have penned this judgment with the fervent hope that it is a prologue to a broader thinking and greater tolerance for the creative field.' The Supreme Court vindicated his line of thinking. This delighted Husain who said, 'At last, the dignity of the Indian contemporary art has been upheld by the Supreme Court as expected.'

His liberal cheerleaders in India were also jubilant at the discomfiture of the saffron brigade which has been inveighing against the artist, and also when Justice Kaul supported Husain. Author (and eventual Congress leader) Shashi Tharoor, for instance, wrote two articles in *The Times of India* in which he quoted Justice Kaul's judgment at length. He hailed the ruling as 'a remarkable charter for artistic freedom in India.' The two articles ran to about 2,000 words, but not once was the name of Taslima Nasreen or Salman Rushdie mentioned. Nor was there any mention of the Danish cartoonist who had made a cartoon of Prophet Mohammad and who was being hounded by Islamists.

Selective indignation

This selective championing of the freedom of expression is obnoxious and hypocritical. Why didn't liberals make their campaign to safeguard the freedom of expression more comprehensive? Why didn't they also take up the cause of other creative people who were hounded by the jihadists? Why didn't they stand up for the 'dignity' of Taslima Nasreen, Rushdie, and the Danish cartoonist?

There are others as well who have suffered for 'hurting the sentiments' of Muslims. For example, in February 2006 Alok Tomar, editor of a Delhi-based Hindi magazine, was arrested for publishing one of the Danish cartoons of Prophet Mohammed. He had to pay Rs 50,000 and provide a personal surety for release.

This time neither Tharoor nor others took up his cause. As far as I know, no judge of the Delhi High Court or of the Supreme Court came to his rescue. There were no protests, candlelight marches, or symposia in Tomar's support. Was it just because his tormentors were Muslims?

There is a great deal of doublespeak on the issue of freedom of expression. The chattering classes cite this freedom when Hindu sensitivities are concerned, but when the Muslims start screaming, they remain silent. Freedom of expression has become a tool to settles scores with the Hindu nationalists. Even common Hindus have noticed this duplicity; unfortunately, they have started paying attention to the arguments of the Shiv Sena and the Bajrang Dal. It seems that Muslim unreasonableness is spawning Hindu intransigence.

Chapter 15

The defamation bugbear

An objection to absolute freedom of expression is that it would lead to chaos. Unrestrained by law, this freedom would degenerate into the licence to malign and vilify opponents. There would be a spurt in cases of defamation. Let us begin with definitions. Merriam-Webster defines 'defame' as 'to harm the reputation of by libel or slander.' Libel is 'a statement or representation published without just cause and tending to expose another to public contempt.' Slander, on the other hand, is 'to make a false spoken statement that causes people to have a bad opinion of someone.'

The operative parts in the definitions of libel and slander are 'without just cause' and 'false spoken statement', respectively. Evidently, freedom of expression, like any other freedom, also entails responsibility on the part of the person who exercises this right. Besides, it is constrained by the Harm Principle that we mentioned in the first chapter. The example quoted there relates to physical harm that may ensue by the abuse of freedom of expression. That principle also covers the harm associated with character assassination.

Free expression becomes libelous only when it shows disdain for just cause to the extent that it ends up wrongly exposing a person or a group of persons to public contempt. Similarly, it becomes slanderous when the spoken words are false. In such cases, the person who defames others cannot and shall not be able to claim that he is just exercising his right to freedom of expression. The adverse remarks he makes, in writing or in speech, should have a verifiable basis.

Two kinds of defamation

There can be two kinds of defamation: outlandish and plausible. If somebody claimed that I killed Mahatma Gandhi, the accusation would be dismissed even by my enemies, as I was not even born when Gandhi was murdered. But the statement that I am a crook masquerading as a journalist is within the realm of possibility. If I am not a crook, the statement is unjust and smears my character. The person who made the statement abused the right to freedom of expression to suit their purpose.

Four points need to be made here. First, rights often entail the danger of their abuse, so the cure is *not the curtailment of rights but of abuse*. Second, if statements are not just cause and false, they can be proved to be so—or at any rate they would never be able to accomplish character assassination. Third, concerted and intense efforts to tarnish upright and honest personalities have failed. Finally, even with severe restrictions on the freedom of expression, innuendo and whisper campaigns are tools widely employed to tarnish the image of opponents.

Consider the Right to Equality, as enshrined in our Constitution. It establishes equality before law: 'The State shall not deny to any person equality before the law or the equal protection of the laws within the territory of India.' It also prohibits 'discrimination on grounds of religion, race, caste, sex or place of birth.' But there are exceptions: 'nothing in this article… shall prevent the State from making any special provision for the advancement of any socially and educationally backward classes of citizens or for the Scheduled Castes and the Scheduled Tribes.' The justification of reservations was, and is, that certain communities, categorised as Scheduled Castes and Scheduled Tribes, faced religious and social discrimination for centuries; therefore, they were given this benefit.

Owing to the abysmal ethical standards in politics and the perverted public discourse, however, the Right to Equality has been abused to bolster petty, divisive policies. A debate on the issue of reservations is beyond the scope of this book, but it must be mentioned that politicians and many intellectuals colluded in perpetuating and expanding the scope of a provision which the founding fathers of Indian Republic intended to be temporary; more communities, the so-called other backward classes or OBCs, were also made the beneficiaries of affirmative action. The perpetuation and expansion of reservations, thus, ended up undermining the very concept of equality. And that too, in the name of equality. Yet, this does not mean that equality as an ideal should be given up. Similarly, the Right to Freedom of Religion—'and all persons are equally entitled to freedom of conscience and the right freely to profess, practise and propagate religion'—is also curtailed; it is also abused to carry out questionable practices.

Then there are Cultural and Educational Rights:

> Any section of the citizens residing in the territory of India or any part thereof having a distinct language, script or culture of its own shall have the right to conserve the same. No citizen shall be denied admission into any educational institutions maintained by the State or receiving aid out of State funds on grounds only of religion, race, caste, language or any of them.

Further, 'all minorities, whether based on religion or language, shall have the right to establish and administer educational institutions of their choice.'

Cultural and Educational Rights were clearly abused when the National Commission for Minority Educational Institutions (NCMEI) granted the minority institution status to Jamia Milia Islamia University on 2 February 2011. This not only meant that the varsity could reserve fifty per cent seats for Muslims but also refuse reservation to Scheduled Castes and Scheduled Tribes students. This is a violation of the letter and spirit of the Constitution, for Cultural and Educational Rights do not mean that taxpayers' money should be used for a religious community. In short, all rights are open to abuse and they have been abused with impunity. Therefore, the argument that freedom of expression can be abused should not be allowed to curtail this right.

As for the statements which are without just cause and false, legal recourse is available to combat character assassination. It can be argued that the legal process in our country is long and cumbersome; by the time the victim gets justice, damage would be done. But then it is the problem with the judicial system, not with the right to freedom of expression. Thousands of people anyway suffer because of the malady in the system.

The politics of maligning

It needs to be emphasised that the danger of character assassination by malicious unfounded charges is highly exaggerated. Consider two high-profile cases, those of former Prime Minister Morarji Desai and Bhartiya Janata Party leader Subramanian Swamy. In his book, *The Price of Power*

(1983), Seymour Hersh made an outlandish accusation: Desai had been paid $20,000 a year by the Central Intelligence Agency during the Johnson and Nixon administrations. Desai was furious at the 'scandalous and malicious lie' and filed a $50-million libel suit against the Pulitzer Award winning journalist. But he was very old, 93, and ailing, to actively pursue the case. Though he did not win the case, the preposterousness of the charge against him was proved. CIA director Richard Helms and Henry Kissinger testified under oath that Desai never received any money from the CIA.

Today decades after his death, Desai's integrity is not questioned by anybody save conspiracy mongers. It is Hersh whose credibility has suffered because of his bizarre and baseless assertion. He has acquired the image of an investigative journalist who is not very careful with facts, his eminence notwithstanding. As he once admitted, 'If the standard for being fired was being wrong on a story, I would have been fired long ago.' He should have been, indeed.

Swamy's case is even more curious: he is perhaps the only person in India who has been consistently and intensely maligned by both the Left and the Right. Left-leaning intellectuals find his pro-market and anti-Islamist views unpalatable; the Sangh Parivar, too, carried out a sustained whisper campaign against him till Atal Bihari Vajpayee, his bête noir, was in the reckoning in the Parivar. Yet despite concerted, well-orchestrated maligning, Swamy has only gained in prominence over the years. At the time of writing these lines, he is the hero of the Parivar.

In politics and public life, insinuations and whisper campaigns have played an important role since time immemorial. No laws, rules, or regulations have ever checked them; nor is it likely to in the foreseeable future. A lot depends on the level of education in society and the richness of public consciousness. In the Muslim world, for instance, the weirdest conspiracy theories about Zionist machinations abound; they cost Imran Khan his marriage as wild rumours were spread about his former wife who is of Jewish extraction. In Western countries where the freedom of expression is seldom compromised, on the other hand, it is difficult to taint a personality without substantial evidence. We, in India, stand somewhere between the Islamic world and the West as far as public credulousness is concerned.

We can conclude by asserting that the fear of unrestrained freedom of expression is grossly exaggerated.

Chapter 16

In love with chains

India is supposed to be a free country, in fact, the world's largest democracy with a Constitution ensuring the freedom of expression. But the reality behind this appearance is not very agreeable: our freedom, though not a sham, is incomplete. Further, we are not only partially free but the sphere of our freedom is also gradually shrinking.

We are partially free; for, as we noted earlier, the Indian Constitution, while ensuring the 'freedom of speech and expression' in Article 19 (a), imposes 'reasonable restrictions' for the maintenance of 'the security of the State, friendly relations with foreign States, public order, decency or morality, or in relation to contempt of court, defamation or incitement to an offence.'

Non-legal restrictions

Apart from the legal Constitutional restrictions, there is the problem of national mood. Not a single day passes without some political party, social organisation, religious group, or a publicity-hungry outfit demanding a ban on some movie, book, exhibition, video remix, *etc.* The ban mania can become endemic, as it has in India in two cases: people, openly or tacitly, support bans; or they are just not bothered. While the former implies that the people have started seeking a variety of chains for their own bondage, the latter suggests that they are casual about being free. In neither case, can we be called a free society.

We certainly do not pass the town-square test as devised by Sharansky. This calls for a brief introduction of the man who has emerged as an evangelist of freedom. Natan (Anatoly) Sharansky was born in the Ukraine and graduated with a degree in mathematics from the Physical Technical Institute in Moscow. His early association with the human rights movement was as an English interpreter for Andrei Sakharov, before emerging in his own right as a foremost dissident and spokesman for the Soviet Jewry movement.

In 1973, Sharansky applied for an exit visa to Israel, but was refused because of 'security' reasons. He remained prominently involved in Jewish refusenik activities until his arrest in 1977. Convicted in 1978 of treason and spying on behalf of the United States, Sharansky was sentenced to thirteen years imprisonment. He spent sixteen months in Moscow's Lefortovo prison, frequently in solitary confinement and in a special 'torture cell', before being transferred to a notorious prison camp in the Siberian Gulag.

During the years of his imprisonment, Sharansky became a symbol of human rights in general and Soviet Jewry in particular. A campaign for his release was waged tirelessly by his wife, Avital, who migrated to Israel immediately after their wedding with the hope that her husband would follow shortly. Intense diplomatic efforts and a public outcry for his release were unsuccessful until 1986, when Sharansky was released as part of an East-West prisoner exchange. Freed on the border of a still-divided Germany, he was met by the Israeli ambassador who presented him immediately with his new Israeli passport under the Hebrew name of Natan Sharansky. He arrived in Israel on 11 February 1986, and was greeted by leading government officials including then Prime Minister Shimon Peres and was given a hero's welcome. He later became a cabinet minister in Israel.

In an interview Sharansky said: 'We can gain some optimism from history.' He cites the example of Japan:

> Truman's advisors were very skeptical about the prospects for democracy in Japan, as were most of the 'experts' of the time. And there were good reasons to be skeptical. This was a country with virtually no exposure to the West for centuries. Japan's rigidly hierarchical society and unique culture was seen as antithetical to democratic life. In fact, when the concept

> of rights was translated into Japan it took a compound word consisting of four characters to express it. But democracy in Japan has been a great success story. Japan is not a Western democracy. The Japanese have kept their traditions, culture and heritage, but they have joined the community of free nations.'

Free societies, fear societies

In Sharansky's scheme of things, there are two kinds of societies: free societies and fear societies:

> Free societies are societies in which the right of dissent is protected. In contrast, fear societies are societies in which dissent is banned. One can determine whether a society is free by applying what we call the 'town-square test.' Can someone within that society walk into the town-square and say what they want without fear of being punished for his or her views? If so, then that society is a free society. If not, it is a fear society.

We are today clearly a fear society and not a free society. Whatever freedom of expression we can boast of today is also getting eroded. The most depressing aspect of this erosion is that it is mostly we, the people of India, who are guilty.

We are behaving like the six prisoners in V. Shantaram's classic *Do Aankhen Barah Haath*. The film's protagonist, played by Shantaram, is an idealist jailor who rehabilitates six dangerous prisoners in an open prison. He wants to reform them through a life of toil and virtue. Having spent years in jail and accustomed to a shackled existence, they are unable to sleep without being chained in the new set-up, so they had to chain themselves up to sleep properly. This scene is the apotheosis of India's affair with freedom.

Freedom can be a difficult bedfellow.

Chapter 17

The cartoonish controversies

In May 2012, a bizarre row animated the political class. Leaders of all parties, especially those belonging to the Dalit community, were incensed that a school textbook—published by the National Council Of Educational Research And Training or NCERT, under the Ministry of Human Resources Development in 2006—carried a cartoon depicting the Constitution drafting committee chairman, B. R. Ambedkar, and former Prime Minister Jawaharlal Nehru. In the cartoon, Nehru is holding a whip, while Ambedkar is driving a snail representing the Indian Constitution. The cartoon was condemned as being derogatory to Ambedkar, who has become like a god for Dalit leaders. Demand was made for its withdrawal from the book, which the government meekly and promptly did, and action against those responsible for its printing.

Human Resources Development Minister Kapil Sibal apologised to the nation for the 'insult' to Ambedkar. The cartoon was published with the approval of the advisors of the textbook committee, Yogendra Yadav and Suhas Palshikar. Both had to quit as advisors of the NCERT text book council. A civil probe was ordered against them and another academic for their 'crime' of having included the cartoon in the textbook. The cartoonist K. Sankar Pillai escaped any penalty: he was long dead.

A publicity stunt

The cartoon was made in 1949, over sixty-two years before it triggered the storm. Nobody, not even Ambedkar, objected to it at that time, or for decades after that. No educationist, school teacher, student, or parent ever found the cartoon offensive. This was not even the case of 'hurting the sentiments', but a Christian-Dalit Parliamentarian from Tamil Nadu, Thirumavalavan, found a convenient way to get publicity by calling it offensive. The entire political spectrum seconded his questionable assertion.

Bahujan Samajwadi Party (BSP) chief Mayawati said:

> This is an insult on Indian democracy. The government should intervene and take strong action against those who are involved in this. If it failed to do so, we will wait for two to three days or else our party will not allow the House to run.

Congress leader and Chairman of the National Commission for Scheduled Castes P.L. Punia, eager to exhibit his pro-Dalit credentials, castigated Sibal and sought an apology from him.

In general, sanctimoniousness scaled a new peak.

A few months later, another cartoonist got into trouble—and not posthumously. A young man based in Mumbai, Aseem Trivedi, drew a cartoon showing Parliament as a toilet; in another, he transformed the national emblem in which wolves replaced the lions and the skull-and-bones warning sign Ashoka Chakra; in yet another, he allegedly depicted the Constitution in a bad light.

The Congress-led government in Maharashtra slapped sedition charges against Trivedi. Roundly slammed for high-handedness, the government later decided to drop the sedition charges. However, the incident exposed fundamental flaws in public discourse. In television discussions, public intellectuals said that Trivedi had 'desecrated' our national symbols, something which is not in good taste. The viewpoint that Trivedi drew crude cartoons may be valid, but the issue was not one of taste; he was not behind bars because he was a bad cartoonist or made a bad one; he was there because his right and his act of drawing such cartoons were considered seditious by the Maharashtra government. At any rate, if good taste were made the criterion of prosecution, most Hindi film directors and TV serial makers would land up in jail along with quite a few television journalists.

The wrong focus

Unfortunately, much of the debate was focused on whether or not Trivedi insulted the nation or people's sentiments, whether he should have been charged with sedition, *etc.* The real issue was not whether or not he showed disrespect to the nation but whether a person ought to be prosecuted even if he showed disrespect to the nation.

As a votary of absolute freedom of expression, my answer is an unequivocal 'no'. Anything can be called indecent, vulgar if there are no universally accepted parameters of determining decency, beauty, *etc.* As I wrote in Chapter I, since there is no universally accepted standard for reality, beauty, decency, and the like, there can be no universally accepted standards of falsehood, ugliness, indecency, *etc.* Therefore, nobody should be put on trial because of their written or spoken words, and their works of art—unless of course there is evidence beyond reasonable doubt that these works causes immediate lawless action.

The principle around which the laws and rules in a liberal democracy are, or should be oriented, is that freedom of expression is absolute. The only condition is that the thought and the expression of it should not harm anybody. But in the wonder that is Indian democracy, we witness something perverse. We live in an era in which bans are demanded at the drop of a hat—and the demands are often acceded to. Equally sad is the acquiescence of the grandees of media and academics to the deceitful and dangerous doctrine that 'freedom does not mean licence.'

In a *Times Now* debate, prominent cartoonist Sudhir Dar urged artists like Trivedi to draw a line between decency and indecency. Dar said that they should not cross the *Lakshman Rekha*, the conventional boundary of correctness. The point is whether or not an artist draws such a line is his prerogative and whether or not to appreciate his works is left to viewers; if people find him vulgar or offensive, then he will lose his standing in the market. The government does not and should not figure in the picture.

When reminded of the famous Voltaire saying, 'I disapprove of what you say, but I will defend to the death your right to say it,' Dar said something to the effect that in our context, the Constitution is so hallowed that nothing should be done that even faintly tends to tarnish, besmirch or belittle it, for it is the Constitution that gives us our fundamental rights, including the freedom of expression.

Inalienable rights

Dar got it wrong. The Constitution neither *gives* us these or other rights, nor did it create them; it merely *registers* them. In fact, no human being, however great, or human agency gives us our rights. This is important to note. The right to freedom, as other rights, is given to us by God or nature; at any rate, it is our inalienable right. These rights were enjoyed by Indians even before the Constitution was made.

When politicians rant against Trivedi, saying that we should not defile the Constitution, they just exhibit egregious hypocrisy, for they and their forebears have amended the Constitution ninety-seven times; many of the original features have been removed; a fundamental right (to property) has been abolished; the freedom of expression has been severely curtailed. So, what Constitution they are talking about? Certainly not the one drafted by the Founding Fathers.

The document that we have today bears little resemblance to the one enacted on 26 January 1950. The concepts that got the biggest beating at the hands of politicians are freedom (of expression as well as economic) and fairness. They have ensured that the Constitution was sapped of its vitality, vibrancy, and essence; what we have today is a shell—a shell of fossilised ideals. We are supposed to worship the idol made of the fossilised ideals. Any aberration in the worship is treated as sacrilege. Trivedi is guilty of such sacrilege.

The emptiness of the shell was made public by the cartoonish controversies.

Chapter 18

Suppositions galore

We respect the freedom of expression but many factors have to be taken into account, pontificate our political masters, most of whom have waged a jihad against liberty. Law & Order cannot be ignored, they claim, adding that human lives are more important than the rights of some aspiring author who fancies himself to be a Voltaire or a Rushdie.

This line of argumentation is flawed on two counts—philosophical and practical. The right to freedom of expression is not just *a* right which we have because some generous personages, in their infinite wisdom and munificence, thought it fit for us and incorporated it in the Constitution during the middle of the twentieth century. As we mentioned earlier, it is an individual's *inalienable* right, prior to and independent of its appearance in any constitution or statute book. Freedom defines a human being. This is not just a legal right or an entitlement that a welfare state has decided to grant us, that can so easily be snatched away.

Since freedom is the essential feature of human beings, it cannot be less important than any other ideal cherished in a liberal democracy. Nobody disputes the importance of Law & Order, but it does not, and should not precede liberty. Actually, there is no contradiction between liberty and peace in the first place; it is erroneous—in fact, mischievous—on the part of politicians and intellectuals to say that liberty needs to be curbed for the sake of peace, or that Law & Order worsens if liberty becomes a license.

Liberty is sacrosanct

Liberty should be viewed as something sacrosanct; it cannot be allowed to be trifled with for the sake of convenience, expedience, or political gains. A man who does not hold something dear worth dying for is just a creature biologically alive, just like any animal. Similarly, a society that does not hold any ideal that is worth any sacrifice lacks vitality, gravitas, and moral compass; it does not deserve to be called liberal or modern; it is indistinguishable from the Stone Age savage hordes who were only a shade better than the beasts surrounding them. Liberty is one ideal a liberal democracy cannot do without. There can be no philosophical, moral, or practical excuses justifying the abrogation or curtailment of freedom of expression in a democracy.

This brings us to the practical aspects of limiting liberty. Do bans and checks on the works of art help maintain Law & Order? Did Rajiv Gandhi's abject capitulation to the demand of Muslim fanatics and craven liberals like Khushwant Singh for the ban of Salman Rushdie's *The Satanic Verses*, result in an improvement in upholding Law & Order? Did the perpetual appeasement of the Thackerays by various regimes at the Centre and in Mumbai make them less violent? There is only one answer to these questions: no. Yet, disingenuous politicians continue to harp on the 'suppose there was a riot' theme... Unfortunately, opinion-makers imbibe these lies as the truths and trot them out at every available forum.

Empirical evidence suggests that there is no correlation between bans and a peaceful public life. India was the first country to ban *The Satanic Verses* (1988). On 13 February 1989, there were anti-Rushdie riots in Srinagar, Jammu and Kashmir, killing one person and injuring over one hundred. On 24 February 1989, a dozen people were killed and forty wounded in a huge anti-Rushdie protest in Bombay, apart from massive loss to property. Despite the fact that the Indian government meekly accepted the diktat of Islamic fundamentalists for the ban of the book, there was violence. Even though there were some disturbances in the US on account of *The Satanic Verses*, there were no killings.

It is fashionable among contemporary liberals to hold something other than Islam responsible for every Islamist outrage. Even in the US, liberals try to find scapegoats: for jihadist terror, it is either Israel or racism. The Obama administration (in)famously held an amateur anti-Islamic video responsible for the murder of its own ambassador in

Libya, while going soft on the attackers with Al-Qaeda links. Obama's officials pontificated about the consequences of 'Islamophobia'. In India, it happens all the time that any negative comment on Islamic practices evokes a strong and sharp reaction. Criticism of regressive Hindu practices is, however, fair game.

A growing tendency

A growing tendency in India is that any individual or group that takes up a retrograde cause finds support from politicians and a large section of intellectuals. Khaps (caste panchayats) trample upon many human rights and civil liberties but politicians rarely oppose them; often they support the medieval institutions. Women are sexually assaulted and raped. Who is held guilty? Not the predators, but the revealing dresses women wear. The victim becomes the villain.

Blaming freedom of expression for certain acts of violence is similar to blaming women for rape. Misogynists claim that women wear skimpy, sexy dresses; this excites men who molest or rape them. Ergo, women wearing short skirts are guilty. Unfortunately, nobody has pointed out that the same men behave perfectly well when in malls and five-star hotels; they know that any indiscretion on their part would have serious consequences because there would be bouncers in to restore order, and the property owner could either be a powerful politician orhave a buddy with the right connections.

The cause of bad behavior is never the attire of women; it is the absence of fear of punishment.

If a filmmaker makes a movie or a novelist tells a story which 'hurts the sentiments' of some people to the extent that they indulge in vandalism and arson, the creative person is held guilty. The truth, however, is that the guilt lies with the vandals and the government agencies that are supposed to uphold Law & Order.

The real scandal

A detailed discussion on administration and Law & Order in the country is beyond the scope of this book but a few comments need to be made. That the political class has made a mess of governance is a truism. After Independence, politicians' obsession with socialism, with the resultant control of the economy and proliferations of entitlements, has had disastrous consequences for the administration. For instance, the 2009 election manifestoes of the two largest parties, the Congress and the Bharatiya Janata Party, did not even mention 'Law & Order'. Therefore, it is not surprising that in our country seventy per cent of milk is adulterated and often made of urea and detergent; decent people are robbed and cheated; cops are interested in collecting protection money rather than upholding the law; outlaws become lawmakers; and nobody is caught if they know the right people in the right places. It's anarchy, except that it is peaceful. Scammers, dacoits, goons, and murderers have no fear of the law because they know that judicial processes take an eternity. As a character played by Hindi film actor and BJP MP Paresh Rawal said in a movie, cops have become thieves and thieves have become ministers. This, then, *is* the real scandal.

It also means that people can afford to express their anger in a violent manner against anything they do not approve of. They know that that the political class is not interested in upholding the rule of law. They can ransack offices, vandalise malls and cinema halls, and thrash anybody they dislike on the pretext that their sentiments were hurt. But the same people behave peacefully when in the UK or the US, despite the fact that the same, hurtful things aboundin foreign countries.

To conclude, the real culprit is not freedom of expression but the absence of the rule of law: this is the correct diagnosis of the situation. Therefore, what is needed is not the curtailment of the freedom of expression but an improvement in Law & Order; indeed a restoration of the rule of law.

Chapter 19

What really encourages rioters

The basic principle of liberal democracy is liberty of thought and action so long as it does not harm others. Restrictions ought to preclude, check, and punish harm, while freedom should be unrestrained. In India, however, it is harm that is unrestrained, whereas liberty is severely curtailed. Our political masters have allowed the system to evolve in this fashion.

We will discuss a few cases underlying this contention which happened in 2012: violence at the Azad Maidan in Mumbai in August; the attitude of the authorities in the controversy surrounding Salman Rushdie's participation at the Jaipur Literary Festival early during that year; and the arrest of two girls over their innocuous remarks on Facebook in November.

A Mumbai-based organisation, Raza Academy, held a protest at the Azad Maidan against the Assam riots and incidents in Myanmar in which many Muslims had reportedly died. The protest turned violent with the demonstrators indulging in arson and assault. They burned vehicles, including those of newspersons, threw stones, attacked policemen, snatched their weapons, molested women constables, and desecrated the Amar Jawan Memorial dedicated to the Unknown Soldier.

Politicised police force

The mob was armed with rods and sticks. The disturbances continued for two hours. The police had to fire in the air and resort to baton-charge to disperse the mob. Two persons died. Many more, including forty-four cops, were injured. This happened primarily because the then Police Commissioner, Arup Patnaik, tried to please his political bosses by protecting the rioting Muslims.

In India, as in many other places in the world, the police react vigorously if they get attacked. But Patnaik wanted to keep his boss, Maharashtra home minister R.R. Patil of the Nationalist Congress Party (NCP) in good humor. Jyoti Punwani, a Mumbai-based journalist and writer, wrote in *The Hindu* (22 October 2012) about the protest organisers' political links. 'Everyone has seen state home minister R.R. Patil of the NCP come calling at the residence of one of them [the rioters], whose brother is an NCP corporator. Another, a known rabble-rouser, heads an organisation involved in another riot in 2006, in which two policemen were lynched in Bhiwandi.' It needs to be mentioned here that Punwani is a typical liberal-secular intellectual for whom the threat of jihad is a 'communal' fiction. Even she could not ignore the virulence of Muslim fanaticism at the Azad Maidan.

Saeed Noori, founder-president of Raza Academy, does not deny his links with Patil, but he had an explanation. 'We go to Patil because he is accessible to us. The Congress ministers don't entertain us,' he told a reporter from *The Times of India* (2 September 2012). Noori had turned 'the Raza Academy into a protest machine.' Protest was the Raza Academy's article of faith, the report says, adding that it has organised protests on a regular basis, some of which resulted in injuries and deaths.

Noori claims to provide a platform to Muslim youth to express themselves but in reality promotes the jihadist agenda. For instance, he resisted Pakistani Sunni scholar Tahirul Qadri's visit to Mumbai in 2011. A cleric, Maulana Mehmood Daryabadi, was quoted by the *TOI* as saying: 'By opposing Qadri, who is on the hit list of the al Qaeda for his moderate views, Raza Academy proved that it is no better than a *dukaan* (shop) which manufactures protests.'

Men like Noori are not an exception but the rule. They are used with utmost brazenness by politicians to further their electoral goals. Fundamentalists are given a free hand in their activities. They promote their regressive agenda, something that does not bother our mainstream parties. Often the objectives of bigots and politicians coincide, as it happened during the Jaipur Literature Festival in January 2012.

Rushdie at the literature festival

On 10 January 2012, Darul Uloom Deoband, a seminary promoting the most rigid form of Islam in Uttar Pradesh, had demanded that the government should not allow Salman Rushdie to attend the festival as he 'had annoyed the religious sentiments of Muslims in the past.' With UP going to polls in a short while, the Congress did not want to upset the Muslim clergy, which wields great influence over the faithful. The situation was therefore allowed to develop in such a way that Rushdie himself opted out of the event. It was decided that he would speak at the festival via video link.

However, the fanatics and their appeasers, the politicians, were not satisfied. Now, they also decided to check Rushdie's tele-speech. William Dalrymple, co-director of the Festival, wrote in *The Guardian* on 26 January 2012:

> Then at about one o'clock, a large number of Muslim activists appeared in the property and gravitated to the back of the lawns where a huge crowd had gathered to hear the video link. Some of them went into the central courtyard of the palace to make their *namaz* (prayers), and according to some reports, the maulana in charge told his followers that if anyone was killed that day they would die a martyr. Then they sought out our producer, Sanjoy Roy, and told him that they were prepared to use any amount of violence in order to stop Rushdie's voice being heard.
>
> Others talked to the press: one told a reporter from the *Times of India* that 'rivers of blood will flow here if they show Rushdie', while the Muslim Manch representative Abdul Salim Sankhla was quoted as saying: 'We will not allow Rushdie to speak here in any form. There will be violent protests if he speaks.' While all this was happening, some of the other activists were turfing school children out of their seats and intimidating festival guests.

> The video link was due to start at 3.45pm. At three o'clock, as Rushdie was already on his way to the television studio, as crowds were gathering, and as the number of activists/thugs was increasing alarmingly…

And how did the political class react to such illiberal abominations? Well, by acting against the writers and organisers. A number of complaints were filed against the authors who read out passages from *The Satanic Verses* at the Festival, as well as the organisers. It was not just the Congress or other 'secular' parties which strengthened the hands of the bigots; the supposedly anti-Muslim Bharatiya Janata Party's minority cell was among the complainants against the accused persons.

The Facebook arrests

It is not that politicians placate only Muslim fanatics; anybody who threatens violence gets a sympathetic hearing. Consider the curious case of two young girls, Shaheen Dhadha (21) and Rainu Shrinivasan (20). Shaheen's 'crime' was her comment on her Facebook page: 'People like Thackeray are born and die daily and one should not observe a *bandh* for that.' The reference was to the unofficial shutdown for three days following the death of Shiv Sena founder-chief Bal Thackeray on 17 November. Her 'accomplice' Renu, committed the unforgivable sin of saying that she 'liked' the comment.

The remark was innocuous. But for the Shiv Sainiks any reference to their god that is less than reverential is tantamount to blasphemy. They filed a police complaint against the girls for 'hurting religious sentiments.' The duo initially faced charges under the draconian Indian Penal Code Section 295A (outraging religious feelings) and Section 66A of Information Technology Act (offensive message through a communication device).

The police high-handedness evoked sharp reactions from a wide spectrum of society. The arrests had sparked an outrage with Press Council of India chief Markandey Katju, a former Supreme Court judge, demanding 'immediate' action against police personnel involved. In an e-mail to Maharashtra Chief Minister Prithviraj Chavan, Katju warned of 'legal consequences' if he failed to take action against the police personnel concerned, said a PTI report: 'Congress said a police case against the girls was "unfortunate" and hoped the Maharashtra government would take remedial measures.'

Even then Telecom and Information Technology minister, Kapil Sibal, a committed enemy of freedom of expression and the social media, was also forced to say that he was 'deeply saddened' by the arrest of the two girls. He went on to add—with the sincerity of a terrorist mouthing pacifist slogans—that the Information Technology Act should not be used to 'throttle dissent.'

The then Janata Party chief Subramanian Swamy condemned the action. 'It is reckless disregard of the Constitution and the fundamental rights by Maharashtra administration to invoke the IPC section 505(2),' he said in a statement. 'I demand that the criminal case be withdrawn and the Chief Minister offer his apologies to the young girl.' The legal experts *The Times of India* spoke to were unanimous in their denunciation of the hounding of the girls. Supreme Court counsel C.A. Sundaram said: 'Freedom comes in expressing something that displeases you.'

'The girls' arrest borders on being ridiculous,' said senior crime law counsel Amit Desai in Mumbai. Moreover, Supreme Court lawyer Sorabh Kirpal commented: 'The police have overreacted and shown complete arbitrariness in effecting the arrest, in such a trivial case, a section meant for grave offences which relate to incitement of communal disharmony.' Advocate N.S. Nappinai, an expert in cyber law, said Section 66A of the Information Technology Act is 'wide in its application'; it is like an 'open minefield of vagueness just waiting to explode and open to abuse. The arrest is just another example of such abuse.' It was the misfortune of the two girls that they tripped on this minefield.

This case again highlighted the fact that while freedom of expression is so grossly trampled upon that violence mostly goes unpunished. Threatened by the Shiv Sainiks, Shaheen apologised for her comment but it did not stop them from allegedly vandalising a hospital owned by her uncle. Owing to the media pressure, the police was forced to arrest nine people, but such arrests are a sham.

A clear message

The incident also sends a message loud and clear: be careful about what you say on the internet. Anything that you say may be misconstrued by anybody, leading to them baying for your blood, sometimes just for cheap publicity. The effect was immediate: the girls were so terrified that they bade adieu to Facebook. Now everybody would be cautious in their remarks. The days of censorship may be over but pre-censorship is creeping in, and the list of thought-crimes increases by the day. The enemies of liberty of all kinds—on the Left and the Right, politicians and publicity seekers—are gaining strength and power. 'If you want a vision of the future, imagine a boot stamping on a human face—forever,' George Orwell wrote in *1984*. The twenty-first century has not been able to dump the dystopia in the dustbin of history. Or if it ever did that,the apocalypse is creeping out of the dustbin, at least in India.

What becomes clear from the above-mentioned incidents is that Law & Order problems are mostly caused by the actions, inactions, and the direct and indirect involvement of politicians. Freedom of expression, just like short skirts in molestation cases, becomes the scapegoat, and leads to demands for 'decency', 'decorum,' *etc.,* in public discourse. Law-abiding citizens are asked to be 'circumspect' (read 'timid') in their writings and speech, whereas troublemakers of various hues are given a long rope, in the same fashion in which women are exhorted to dress properly while the ruffians are allowed to go scot-free.

Chapter 20

'World-class freedom'

There was a time when Indian politicians promised to transform their cities into London, Paris, Shanghai. Then came the obsession with everything 'world-class'. Now, we are promised world-class townships, world-class infrastructure, world-class airports, world-class roads. The question is: why not world-class freedom and governance?

Let us begin with governance. Actually, good governance is the difference between civilisation and barbarianism; it is the bulwark against evil. As British philosopher and statesman Edmund Burke said: 'All that is necessary for the triumph of evil is for good men to do nothing.' In India, the situation is worse. It is not only the good people who are mute spectators to the downward spiral in the state of affairs; even those who are duty-bound to combat unconscionable practices, and are empowered to do that, do nothing. Former prime minister Manmohan Singh is a prime example—a good man, honest, very educated, very decent, but not very upright; despite occupying the most powerful office in the country for ten years (2004-14), he turned a blind eye to the corruption of his ministers, the deterioration of Law & Order, the machinations of lunatic fringe on the Left. Mahatma Gandhi was no better. As we shall see later, he played a key role in preparing the ground for the introduction of the illiberal Section 295A of the Indian Penal Code. But other politicians, too, tend to ignore the most vital aspects of life. One such relates to the widespread adulteration of edibles; the most extreme instance of it is synthetic milk.

Actually, it is nothing but mass murder. Having become endemic in the country, especially in North India, since the early 1990s, a number of instances have been reported by the media in considerable detail, yet few people (certainly not those in the government) are bothered.

Callous administration

A public interest litigation (PIL) had to be filed to make our politicians and bureaucrats move. In response to the public PIL filed by a group of citizens led by an Uttarakhand-based pontiff, the Supreme Court issued notices to the Centre in 2012 and Delhi, Uttar Pradesh, Uttarakhand, Rajasthan and Haryana governments.

In February 2012, the Food Safety Standards Authority of India had stated that at the national level, '68.4 per cent of the samples were not found to be conforming to the FSS [Food Safety Standards] Regulations.' Moreover, 'fourteen per cent of the samples were found to be non-conforming because of the presence of traces of detergent.'

It is depressing that a writ of mandamus is needed to make the administration do what it should have been doing anyway on its own to check this menace, for the criminality of making and selling synthetic milk is beyond reasonable doubt. Milkmen in our country have been mixing water with milk since time immemorial but this traditional adulteration is nothing compared to the hideous innovation called synthetic milk. While the milk mixed with water is less nutritious, synthetic milk is actually no milk, it is a lethal concoction of vegetable refined oil, detergents, urea, fertilizers, and other inedible substances.

The Indian Council for Medical Research and medical experts has warned of the hazardous health effects of consuming such milk. These include food poisoning, other gastrointestinal complications, liver damage, kidney impairment, heart problems, cancer, and even death. They have also pointed out that the effect on children would be more severe. There are no studies or estimates available as to how many people have died because of synthetic milk and how many have suffered. But why have governments not done anything to eradicate the evil?

One reason was corruption. According to a 2010 estimate, while one litre of pure milk was usually sold for Rs 30, synthetic milk fetched Rs 20 per litre. However, the cost of the latter was just Rs 2. With such huge margins, the people involved in the business are left with enough money to bribe the local authorities and police.

Banality of evil

The situation brings to the mind the phrase 'banality of evil,' which was coined by Hannah Arendt. Her 1963 work, *Eichmann in Jerusalem: A Report on the Banality of Evil*, asserts that ordinary people, rather than some monstrous Dr No or Mogambo, are responsible for great evils like the Holocaust. They carry out unspeakable atrocities under the assumption that such activities are normal.

This brings us to the second and more important reason for the menace: in the Indian context, it is not some totalitarian state that has occasioned the mass murder; the total abdication of essential duties by the state is responsible for the crime. A political class consumed by the ideology of entitlements has little patience for such matters. This ideology reduces statecraft to an exercise in selling dreams to stay in power. Unsurprisingly, the conventional duties of the government like administration and Law & Order get short shrift.

As we noted earlier, the term 'Law & Order' does not appear in the 2009 manifestoes of the country's two largest parties, the Congress and the Bharatiya Janata Party. It is difficult to remember a time when a serious, informed, and meaningful political debate took place over issues like Law & Order and administrative, police, and judicial reforms. From the politicians' perspective, these issues are not sexy; entitlements are. Politicians don't realise that governance precedes welfarism, that the essential duties of the state cannot be efficaciously replaced with poverty alleviation or job generation schemes, that populism is no substitute for administration. In fact, the success of these schemes presupposes the existence of functional administration. A welfare state is still a state and a failed state cannot become a welfare state.

The things that were thought to exist in the realms of startling philosophical theses and the pages of history have come to haunt us—and that too, is normal. The normal has become frightening. That politicians and bureaucrats would build fortunes is a truism; that the job of police is to provide security to VIPs, serve the interests of the ruling party, and collect *hafta* (weekly bribes) is an accepted and tolerated practice.

When state abdicates

In Dostoevsky's novel *The Brothers Karamazov*, a character says something to the effect that 'without God... all things are lawful...'. I don't know whether or not God exists but one thing is indubitable: in the absence of state or when the state does not carry out its essential duties, everything becomes permissible. Even synthetic milk, contaminated vegetables, and fruits and spurious medicine. We live in a country where a lot is wrong. This is a country where the rule of law has ceased to exist. Statecraft has been reduced to a concoction of claptrap, jamborees, and populism; governance has become a joke.

Such being the realities of our polity, it is not surprising that the basic goal of liberal democracy—harmonising liberty with order—has been forgotten. Owing to the continuous erosion of the underpinnings of a civilisation, Law & Order as well as liberty are under perpetual threat. To quote Burke again:'Among a people generally corrupt liberty cannot long exist.' The corruption in our case is not just political and administrative but also intellectual and moral. As a nation, we are not able to fathom the magnitude of threats—the deleterious impact on liberty is incalculable.

Chapter 21

Ban on pornography is illiberal

In March 2014, Punjabi singer Jasbir Jassi urged the Supreme Court and the Ministry of Information and Broadcasting to check the 'vulgar lyrics' of many popular songs. Assuming that his action emanates from his genuine concern for society, and not from jealousy for fellow singers, his move was fraught with the dangers of further encroachment on the freedom of expression. He seemed to have forgotten the fable of the Monkey and Two Cats.

Many people bemoan vulgar songs, double entendre, bad language, *etc.*, in cinema, on television, and in popular culture in general. The lament is that such things have a bad influence on children and are a nuisance when watched in the company of the family. To that extent, the complaint is valid. Children should not be exposed to obscenity; broadcasters need to ensure this; and, if they don't, the authorities are well within their rights to restrain TV channels.

The same goes with pornography: it should be strictly out of reach of kids. As for child pornography, the makers and purveyors should be charged with nothing short of rape, because sex with any child is rape and anybody making it happen or benefiting from it deserves no leniency.

However, pornography itself—when the participants are adults and are working on their own volition—should not be banned. The reason being that any activity involving consenting adults that does not harm others has to be allowed; proscription will militate against the spirit of liberal democracy. However offensive blue films and girlie magazines may appear to be to some people, pornography still has a right to exist so long as no coercion is involved.

When the twain meet

But, interestingly, there seems to be a consensus between Leftists and some Rightists over the ban on pornography. Most feminists and Leftists describe pornography in their favourite jargon: it exploits women; it harms women during production of pornographic material; women are reduced to sex objects; sexual violence against females is encouraged; it propagates hatred of women; a feminist (Gail Dines) called pornography 'the perfect propaganda piece for patriarchy.' All these are myths, for women in pornography opt for this career; in fact, many of them chose it in their forties. They even have their own websites. In no way are they coerced into the profession. This is not to say coercion has been absent, but in such cases it is coercion rather than pornography that needs to be acted against.

As for harm during production, this is an occupational hazard—and for both, women as well as men; at any rate, now studios are very cautious about sexually transmitted diseases and HIV-AIDS. Further, there is no cause-and-effect relationship between pornography, on the one hand, and sexual violence against women and hatred of women, on the other.

On the Right, Irving Kristol wrote a celebrated essay, 'Pornography, Obscenity, and the Case for Censorship,' which made a case against pornography. Kristol, the founder of neo-conservatism, wrote: 'The purpose of any political regime is to achieve some version of the good life and the good society. It is not at all difficult to imagine a perfectly functioning democracy which answers all questions except one—why should anyone of intelligence and spirit care a fig for it?' His entire case is based on 'the good life and the good society.'

People in every society do envision 'the good life and the good society'; but it is done unconsciously, as unconsciously as the conservative mind 'incarnates concrete traditions' (Peter Viereck). But this gives rise to a number of questions. Is there, or even can there be, a consensus among all people about the vision of the good life and the good society? Further, should it be the 'purpose of any political regime' to achieve such a version? And can there ever be a consensus on the means to achieve such version?

Would it not lead to some or other sort of social engineering and, eventually, totalitarianism? In fact, such an endeavour would be a threat to the open society, in the present as well as in the future. No matter the nature of this endeavour, rightist or leftist, the results will always be disastrous.

Sushma's Taliban vision

Let us see what a rightist vision does in the Indian context: Former Information and Broadcasting Minister Sushma Swaraj, who now holds the foreign portfolio, wants to guard our morals, as also the glorious Hindu culture against the onslaught of the decadent Western culture. Posing as Lady Savonarola, she ensured thatseveral TV advertisementswere taken off the air as they threatened to 'pollute our culture'—whatever that means). She also launched a campaign against Fashion TV, the channel devoted to fashion trends. Given a chance, she would become the Big Sister, deciding what women should wear and men should watch, what people should do, when they freak out.

Unfortunately, she is not alone in the ruling dispensation, comprising Hindu nationalists, championing such regimentation. Unless checked vigorously, the Sanghis will start coming up with more and more stupid diktats: what to wear, which movies to watch, which ads and serials to ban, which books to prescribe and which ones to proscribe, and so on—they will continue to sermonise on each and every such issue. And they would leave no stone unturned to effect their sermons. The saffron brigade feels bad when young men and women exchange cards on Valentine's Day; they don't have compunctions in physically assaulting young couples who celebrate Valentine's Day. The brigade is the enemy of open society.

In other words, whenever there is an endeavour, especially state-sponsored endeavour, to achieve any 'version of the good life and the good society', the consequences are unpleasant. It is indeed ironical that Kristol, who so brilliantly portrayed the spiritual malaise and intellectual desertification in communist countries, should argue in favour of the conscious and state-dependent efforts to bring realise the good life and the good society. For such efforts encroach upon the autonomy of the society and culture.

As American conservative thinker Frank S Mayer wrote, '[C]ommunity conceived as a principle of social order prior and superior to the individual person, can justify any oppression of individual persons so long as it is carried out in the name of "community", or of its agent, the state.'

Principle of collectivism

Such a conception is the foundation of collectivism; it remains the principle of collectivism even though the neo-conservatives would prefer a congeries of communities based upon locality, occupation, belief, caste, class, traditional ties, *etc.*, to the totalising and leveling national or international community which is the goal of Left collectivists.

Whatsoever be the nature of collectivism—Rightwing or Leftwing, conservative or progressive, nationalist or radical, small or big—the consequences are mostly unpleasant, ending up further empowering government and, concomitantly, fettering the individual. The government and its agencies assume the role of the inquisitor and the arbiter in the process. When it is not censorship, it is a public outcry for ban or violent demonstrations. And who will decide whether or not to ban? Some clique of politicians or bureaucrats who invariably have their own agendas, vested interests, and idiosyncrasies.

Demands of censorship and ban on various works of fiction and art are rooted in the postulate that there do exist blueprints for society, art, literature, and culture—and not just some version of the good life and the good society; the obscene and the objectionable are those expressions, forms, and discourses which do not conform to the well-established canons and generally accepted norms. Needless to say, it is the collectivities such as political parties, communities, socio-cultural organisations, and the most powerful institution, the state, that determine the legitimate and the illegitimate, the sober and the obscene, the progressive and the regressive.

In April 2014, the government rejected the demand of a ban on Internet pornography on practical grounds. The Secretary of the Department of Telecommunications (DoT) informed the Supreme Court that though it is possible to issue direction for blocking pornographic websites, it is not feasible to black out all such websites due.

In his affidavit in the apex court, he said: 'As publication and transmission of pornographic material (excluding child pornography which is illegal almost everywhere in the world) is legal in these countries, it is not possible to take actions against entities operating such servers under Indian laws.' The court was hearing a public interest litigation(PIL) demanding proscription of websites in the country.

He pointed out that it was 'technologically not feasible to monitor the contents' since it would involve human intervention, which is bound to increase the delay in transmission and would consequently slow down the internet. 'As all forms of data, audio, video, text, images, *etc.*, are transmitted together, it will not only introduce large delay in the transmission of forms of data but may also adversely affect the normal audio communications made through Internet telephony. The entire traffic from the websites, emails, electronic and financial transactions, *etc.*, will have to be examined during the process,' the affidavit said (But, after Swaraj's party came to office in May 2014, the government again tried to ban pornography).

Morality mobsters

It would have been better that if the government had said that censorship of the net, even for the purpose of stopping pornography, would be illiberal. But even its refusal on practical grounds was laudable, for these are indeed dangerous times for writers, scholars, filmmakers, and other creative people in India. Books are getting banned or pulped, movies heavily censored, and song lyrics changed at the behest of government, politicians, publicity seekers, and morality mobsters(Yes, this is a better term than 'moral cops'; why bestow a semblance of legitimacy on these thugs?). They use a variety of tricks to curtail freedom. Jassi has not covered himself in glory by joining the mob that is the enemy of liberty.

The first premise of the morality mobsters is that they represent us, the people of India. The second is that they, and only they, know what is good and what is bad for us. And the third is that we are so stupid and impressionable that we can be swayed by a bad film, a ribald song, or a tendentious book; we need constant guidance so that we do not swerve from the Good Path which, of course, only the self-appointed champions of morals know.

All these premises are wrong. Morality mobsters don't represent the people of India; they only present their own prejudices, ignorance, and intolerance in their opposition to a creative work. Actually, they are themselves fascistic as they want to impose their own perverted views on others. They are grossly immoral on their own. So, the mobsters can't decide what's good or bad for others. Finally, we, the people, are neither stupid nor impressionable. We are individuals who have been given, by God or nature, a free will so that we can choose whatever we want. If we can choose who would be right to govern us, to make laws that could send any of us to the gallows, to protest our life and liberty, and to keep our national borders; if we can choose our professions, spouses, the schools for our children, and the persons to interact with; if we can choose the investment instruments on which our future would depend; if we can take a myriad of decisions in our everyday life—well, then, we are also capable enough to know which movie we should watch and which book to read. We don't need any advisory from cantankerous groups over these matters. We can choose.

The choice may be right or wrong, beneficial or harmful, legal or illegal, but it is the individual alone who is supposed to choose in a modern, liberal society. If the choice harms another individual or violates the law of the land, the offender would be punished; if the choice is made imprudently in an investment, the individual would suffer the erosion of his capital. Similarly, if a person chooses vulgar songs over, say, Begum Akhtar, he would grow into an oaf—and would be known as one. If somebody wished to live a life following all the rituals and superstitions of his faith, his social and economic status may remain low. But every individual has a right to be uncultured and superstitious, as he also has a right to be refined and rational.

So, Jasbir Jassi has a right to choose which songs he wants to sing and which ones to avoid. In an interview on 25 March 2014 in *The Times of India*, he said:

> I recently got three lines removed from a song in a Nikhil Advani film. *Woh two-three lines itni kharab thi ki mujhe sharam aa gayi* [three or four lines were so bad that I felt embarrassed] I said I can't sing them. This fight is affecting my work as well, but at least I have the satisfaction that I am doing something good.

This is laudable because this is a moral stand: he finds something repulsive, so he refrains from it despite professional losses. But his petition against vulgar songs smacks of sanctimoniousness. As the American author Thomas Sowell wrote:

> How do you tell morality from sanctimoniousness? For one thing, morality is hard and sanctimoniousness is easy. Anyone who has succumbed to temptation, and then felt deeply ashamed long afterwards, knows how hard morality can be. Sanctimoniousness is easy. There are editorial writers who are sanctimonious every day of the week, without any visible sign

> of fatigue. As far as they are concerned, those who disagree with them are not merely in error, but in sin. Morality means being hard on yourself. Sanctimoniousness means being easy on yourself—and hard on others.

Therefore, Jassi's second stand—as that of the morality mobsters whom he wishes to join—is sanctimonious. And when sanctimoniousness prevails, the only people who get empowered are politicians, officers of the state, and the enemies of liberty. Today, Jassi finds the lyrics of YoYo Honey Singh crude; tomorrow, somebody else—a professional rival, some personal enemy, or just an idle publicity-seeker—may find something wrong with Jassi's songs. The boot would be on the other foot. And the same high and mighty of the land would then judge Jassi who now wants to judge the likes of Honey Singh.

So, the likes of Jassi should not monkey around with the dangerous game of moral policing. In this game, the artist is always the loser and the state the winner. He should remember that cats always lose and the monkey always wins.

Chapter 22

The permanence of Section 66A

India's Supreme Court struck down Section 66A of the Information Technology Act 2005 on 24 March 2015, calling it a 'draconian' provision and a violation of the right of free speech. Introduced in 2009, Section 66A intended to proscribe anything that was 'grossly offensive.' According to the section:

Any person who sends, by means of a computer resource or a communication device—

(a) any information that is grossly offensive or has menacing character; or

(b) any information which he knows to be false, but for the purpose of causing annoyance, inconvenience, danger, obstruction, insult, injury, criminal intimidation, enmity, hatred or ill will, persistently by making use of such computer resource or a communication device; or

(c) any electronic mail or electronic mail message for the purpose of causing annoyance or inconvenience or to deceive or to mislead the addressee or recipient about the origin of such messages, shall be punishable with imprisonment for a term which may extend to three years and with fine.

A Bench of Justices consisting of J. Chelameswar and Rohinton F. Nariman, struck down the section in its entirety 'being violative of Article 19(1)(a)and not saved under Article 19(2).' Article 19(2) of the Constitution of India pertains to the restrictions on the freedom of expression as defined in Article 19(1)(a). Article 19(2) says: 'Nothing in sub clause (a) of clause (1) shall affect the operation of any existing law, or prevent the State from making any law, in so far as such law imposes reasonable restrictions on the exercise of the right conferred by the said subclause in the interests of the sovereignty and integrity of India, the security of the State, friendly relations with foreign States, public order, decency or morality or in relation to contempt of court, defamation or incitement to an offence.' As I mentioned earlier, 'reasonable restrictions' themselves militate against the spirit of Article 19(1)(a), especially in matters related to as subjective as decency and morality.

Section 66A, however, was so obnoxious that it could not pass the reasonable-restrictions test. As the Supreme Court said, 'It is clear that Section 66A arbitrarily, excessively and disproportionately invades the right of free speech and upsets the balance between such right and the reasonable restrictions that may be imposed on such right.'

The apex court said that there are three concepts which are fundamental in understanding the reach of this most basic human right:

> The first is discussion, the second is advocacy, and the third is incitement. Mere discussion or even advocacy of a particular cause howsoever unpopular is at the heart of Article 19(1)(a). It is only when such discussion or advocacy reaches the level of incitement that Article 19(2) kicks in. It is at this stage that a law may be made curtailing the speech or expression that leads inexorably to or tends to cause public disorder or tends to cause or tends to affect the sovereignty and integrity of India, the security of the State, friendly relations with foreign States, *etc.*

The Supreme Court underlined the blurred distinction between discussion, advocacy, *etc.,* on the one hand, and incitement, on the other. For Section 66A to come into play, the information sent has to be annoying, inconvenient, grossly offensive, *etc.*, but 'no distinction is made between mere discussion or advocacy of a particular point of view which maybe annoying or inconvenient or grossly offensive to some' and 'incitement by which such words lead to an imminent causal connection with public disorder, security of State, *etc.*'

The government used all tricks to perpetuate Section 66A; one such related to the medium, the internet itself. Additional Solicitor General

Tushar Mehta urged a relaxed standard of reasonableness of restriction because the internet differs from other mediums on several grounds. He said that 'the reach of print media is restricted to one state or at the most one country while internet has no boundaries and its reach is global.' Further, 'the recipient of the free speech and expression used in a print media can only be literate persons while internet can be accessed by literate and illiterate both since one click is needed to download an objectionable post or a video.'

Then there was the danger of 'morphing of images, change of voices and many other technologically advance (*sic*) methods to create serious potential social disorder can be applied.' By the medium of internet, the government counsel said, 'rumours having a serious potential of creating a serious social disorder can be spread to trillions (*sic*) of people without any check which is not possible in case of other mediums.'

Apart from bad English and poor general knowledge (there are 1,000 billions in one trillion and world population is seven billion), the fallaciousness of the arguments showed the keenness of the Bharatiya Janata Party government to continue the draconian section. The BJP, it may be mentioned, had expressed its unhappiness over Section 66A when it was in Opposition, but it fought tooth and nail to save the vile provision when it entered office. It is another matter that, as we shall see later, the party greeted the Supreme Court decision invalidating the section with considerable enthusiasm; the Congress, which had introduced the section in the first place, also welcomed the verdict.

The apex court, however, dismissed the government's stand, saying 'we do not find anything in the features outlined by the learned Additional Solicitor General to relax the Court's scrutiny of the curbing of the content of free speech over the internet.'

The court saw mischief in equating defamation, which is objective in nature and is acrime, with annoyance or inconvenience, which is subjective and not a crime:

> It will be noticed that for something to be defamatory, injury to reputation is a basic ingredient. Section 66A does not concern itself with injury to reputation. Something may be grossly offensive and may annoy or be inconvenient to somebody without at all affecting his reputation. It is clear therefore that the Section is not aimed at defamatory statements at all.

On the issue of obscenity, the Supreme Court said:

> Section 66A cannot possibly be said to create an offence which falls within the expression 'decency' or 'morality' in that what may be grossly offensive or annoying under the Section need not be obscene at all—in fact the word 'obscene' is conspicuous by its absence in Section 66A.

The court also came down heavily on the vagueness of the language of Section 66A. Citing a British case in which different judges had viewed offence differently, India's Supreme Court said:

> If judicially trained minds can come to diametrically opposite conclusions on the same set of facts it is obvious that expressions such as 'grossly offensive' or 'menacing' are so vague that there is no manageable standard by which a person can be said to have committed an offence or not to have committed an offence. Quite obviously, a prospective offender of Section 66A and the authorities who are to enforce Section 66A have absolutely no manageable standard by which to book a person for an offence under Section 66A.

The imperative of reasonableness

There is another important aspect which the Supreme Court did not mention but needs elucidation. The restrictions on freedom of expression have to be *reasonable* and there are should be *reasonable* grounds to believe that the expression in question can harm national security, jeopardise friendly relations with foreign countries, disturb public order, offend decency or morality, contemn court, lead to defamation, or occasion incitement to an offence. Nowhere is it mentioned that *offending the feelings* or *hurting the sentiments* of somebody can be a ground for curtailment of the freedom of expression.

The grounds restricting the freedom of expression have to be reasonable, and not sentimental, not only because it is the Constitutional position, but also because reasons can be objectively debated; sentiments can't be. The imperatives of law and public administration, on the other hand, are moulded by objective realities. Poetry is to sentiments and subjectivity what political philosophy is to statecraft, jurisprudence, and objectivity.

The Supreme Court did not posit these arguments, but it highlighted the fact that the loose language of Section 66A—necessitated by its emphasis on offensiveness—would have a 'chilling effect' on the freedom of expression:

> Information that may be grossly offensive or which causes annoyance or inconvenience are undefined terms which take into the net a very large amount of protected and innocent speech. A person may discuss or even advocate by means of writing disseminated over the internet information that may be a view or point of view pertaining to governmental, literary, scientific or other matters which may be unpalatable to certain sections of society. It is obvious that an expression of a view on any matter may cause annoyance, inconvenience or may be grossly offensive to some. A few examples will suffice. A certain section of a particular community may be grossly offended or annoyed by communications over the internet by 'liberal views'—such as the emancipation of women or the abolition of the caste system or whether certain members of a non-proselytising religion should be allowed to bring persons within their fold who are otherwise outside the fold. Each one of these things may be grossly offensive, annoying, inconvenient, insulting or injurious to large sections of particular communities and would fall within the net cast by Section 66A. In point of fact, Section 66A is cast so widely that virtually any opinion on any subject would be covered by it, as any serious opinion dissenting with the mores of the day would be caught within its net. Such is the reach of the Section and if it is to withstand the test of constitutionality, the chilling effect on free speech would be total.'

Such was the intensity of the government's desire to persist with Section 66A that it went to the extent of saying that even if the Supreme Court found the provision was bad, the government should be allowed to keep it because it was 'committed to free speech.' The Additional Solicitor General said that even if Section 66A is capable of being abused, it is otherwise valid. The Supreme

Court said: 'He further assured us that this government was committed to free speech and that Section 66A would not be used to curb free speech, but would be used only when excesses are perpetrated by persons on the rights of others.' If Section 66A is otherwise invalid, the court went on, it cannot be saved by an assurance from the Additional Solicitor General that it will be administered in a reasonable manner:

> Governments may come and Governments may go but Section 66A goes on forever. An assurance from the present Government even if carried out faithfully would not bind any successor Government. It must, therefore, be held that Section 66A must be judged on its own merits without any reference to how well it may be administered.

So, the Supreme Court forced the government to discard Section 66A. The verdict was a slap in the face of the government—in fact, of the entire political class. Everybody took the slap smilingly, though. The BJP government welcomed the judgment, saying that it 'resolutely stood up against the censorship and blocking on social media done by' the previous, Congress-led regime. Of course, the BJP government did not mention how disgracefully it had argued in the Supreme Court for the continuance of Section 66A.

The Congress was even more hypocritical and shameless. Kapil Sibal, who had brought in the obnoxious section, called it 'a welcome judgment.' He is an eminent lawyer, but he could found 'nothing unconstitutional about the section'; all problems arising out of it were because of its 'misuse' by the police.

P. Chidambaram, another Congress leader, well-known lawyer, and Sibal's Cabinet colleague when Section 66A was introduced, also woke up to the fact that 'the section was poorly drafted and was vulnerable.' Unfortunately for the victims of Section 66A—they were a legion, many of them harassed by politicians and their henchmen—this realisation came to Chidambaram only after the vile provision was scrapped. In fact, his son, Karti, was one of the beneficiaries of Section 66A; he used it to settle scores with a businessman who had the temerity of accusing him of corruption.

But it was not just hypocrites who welcomed the Supreme Court judgment; there were people who were genuinely happy. Even during the arguments stage, the case had become a cause célèbre; the verdict was widely reported in the media and commented upon by experts and others. There was scarcely any adverse remark about the judgment.

That, perhaps, is the solitary redeeming feature. As we saw earlier, the political class is not committed to protecting the freedom of expression at any cost. But the reverse is also true: it is *also* not committed to destroying liberty; it is completely amoral and Machiavellian, not committed to any principles, good or bad. A rap on the knuckles by the judiciary was all that was needed to make our political masters throw away the obnoxious section.

Yet, the danger to free speech can scarcely be overemphasised; some lackey of some minister is always working to silence the criticism and lampooning of his boss; he will always come up with some pretext, and considerable sophistry, to peddle some legal provision to throttle freedom of expression. The pretext would be couched in politically correct phraseology—respect for elected representatives and democratically-elected government, deference for religious communities and their beliefs, gender sensitivity, image of the nation, decreasing negativity in society, and so on. Incidentally, the rationale offered by the initiators of Section 66A was on similar lines; exasperated by the castigation of Sonia Gandhi—who was the *de facto* boss during the ten-year Congress rule (2004-14)—and her family, her loyalists wanted to keep the Dynasty immune to criticism. Her rule ended nonetheless, but Section 66A outlived it.

In short, the citizens of heightened consciousness have to be on their guard all the time. For, as they say, constant vigilance is the price of liberty.

Chapter 23

What West does and what we do when freedom is under fire

It would be instructive to study the general reaction to the assault on freedom of expression in India and in the West. We shall focus on two instances of violence, which have had a profound bearing on liberty—the *Rangila Rasul* case in our country before Independence and the killing of *Charlie Hebdo* journalists in recent times.

Rangila Rasul (meaning Colourful or Promiscuous Prophet), a book published in Punjab during the early 1920s, is an explicit account of the marriages and sex life of Prophet Muhammad. In Punjab there was considerable tension between Arya Samaj and Muslims. An Arya Samajist wrote the book under a pseudonym. The publisher, Mahashe Rajpal of Lahore, was also a prominent member of the Arya Samaj. Apparently, the book was a response from the Hindu community against a pamphlet published by a Muslim which showed Sita as a prostitute.

Muslims raised a hue and cry; they pressured Rajpal to reveal the name of the author, but he refused. As a consequence, he was arrested, prosecuted under Section 153A, and convicted by the trial court. The Lahore High Court, however, set aside the conviction. Justice Dalip Singh's logic while exonerating Rajpal was impeccable, and in the best traditions of liberalism:

> It seems to me that that section [153A] was intended to prevent persons from making attacks on a particular community as it exists at the present time and was not meant to stop polemics against deceased religious leaders, however scurrilous and in bad taste such attacks might be. For instance, if the fact that Mussalmans resent attacks on their Prophet was to be the measure of whether S 153A applied or not then *an historical work in which the life of the prophet was considered and Judgment passed on his character by a serious historian might come within the definition of S 153A.* I am unable to hold that S 153A was meant or was intended to prevent all adverse discussions of the life and character of a deceased religious leader. (emphasis in the original).

Needless to say, Justice Singh's judgment infuriated the Muslims. Neeti Nair said:

> The case was decided on 4 May 1927. It was almost three weeks before a full copy of the judgment was made available to newspapers although the fact of Rajpal's acquittal was widely known soon after. The only immediate reaction came from the pulpit of the Jama Masjid in Delhi: Maulana Mohamed Ali predicted that 'very serious consequences' would follow the acquittal. The various reviews of the judgment that were eventually published in the press did follow a communal pattern: true to form, Hindu papers commended the acquittal while Muslim papers condemned the judgment. *The Muslim Outlook* took a particularly strong position recommending that an enquiry be conducted into the circumstances under which Dalip Singh wrote his judgment and also that the judge, now damned as 'incompetent', resign.'[8]

Gandhi adds fuel to the fire

While the Muslims were furious, Mahatma Gandhi was also upset with the publication of *Rangila Rasul.* It was the aftermath of the failure of the

8 Pragmatism, and the Making of Section 295A of the Indian Penal Code, 2013, Indian Economic Social History Review

Non-Cooperation-Khilafat Movement (1919-24). He strove to achieve two objectives from the movement: first, to organise all Indians against British rule, and second, to cement Hindu-Muslim unity. He surely failed to attain the second objective, which was not surprising, for the Muslims were more interested in perpetuating the retrograde, bigoted, misogynistic, and tyrannical Caliph in Turkey, than driving out imperialists from their own land and achieving self-rule. At best, the Congress-Khilafat partnership was a tactical alliance that got crushed under the weight of its own contradictions.

But Gandhi was still hopeful of winning back the Muslim support, despite having received considerable vituperation from Khilafat leaders. One of them, Mohammed Ali, soon after the end of the Khilafat movement commented: 'However pure Mr. Gandhi's character may be, he must appear to me, from the point of religion, inferior to any Mussalman even though he be without character.' One can imagine how Ali must have viewed other Hindus.

Yet, Gandhi was besotted with the idea of Hindu-Muslim unity, an obsession that lasted till the end of his life, an obsession that blinded him to the truth of a nation, the Muslim nation, that wanted to secede from the Indian civilisation. But the truth finds a way to express itself, whatever experiments one may carry out to suppress it. Pakistan did come into being, though after the death of hundreds of thousands and the displacement of millions—both Hindus and Muslims. But that is another story.

What is pertinent from our perspective is the fact that Gandhi slammed *Rangila Rasul*. In an article, 'Hindu–Muslim Unity' (*Young India*, 19 June 1924), he wrote:

> A friend has sent me a pamphlet called *Rangila Rasul* written in Urdu. The author's name is not given. It is published by the Manager, Arya Pustakalaya, Lahore. The very title is highly offensive. The contents are in keeping with the title. I cannot, without giving offense to the reader's sense of the fine, give the translation of some of the extracts. I have asked myself *what the motive possibly could be in writing or printing such a book except to inflame passions*. Abuse and caricature of the Prophet cannot wean a Musalman from his faith, and it can do no good to a Hindu who may have doubts about his own belief. As a contribution therefore to the religious propaganda work, it has no value whatsoever. The harm it can do is obvious.' (Emphasis in the original).

According to Kapil Malhotra, my first publisher and a grandson of Rajpal, 'The passions inflamed by the *Rangila Rasul* controversy had quelled by the time Gandhi reacted. His remarks reignited the row, making it nationwide.' Gandhi's statement almost countenanced the Muslim position. Emboldened by his stand, Muslim fanatics murderously campaigned against Rajpal. They succeeded in instigation to such an extent that an illiterate teenager from Lahore called Ilm-ud-Din ended up killing Rajpal. Obviously, he had not read the book, or any other book. It is an interesting story how this boy, son of a carpenter, took the decision to assassinate a man he didnot know.

Once, while passing near Masjid Wazir Khan, he saw a huge, agitated crowd shouting slogans against Rajpal. A rabble-rouser was working up the mob: 'Oh Muslims! The devil Rajpal has sought to dishonour our beloved Prophet Muhammed (S.A.W.) by his filthy book!' Ilm-ud-Din is said to have decided then and there to kill the publisher. He bought a dagger and, on 6 September 1929, stabbed Rajpal to death. He was arrested and tried; Muhammad Ali Jinnah fought his case on a special request from the poet Iqbal, the spiritual founder of Pakistan. Ilm-ud-Din, though only nineteen, did not show any remorse; instead he claimed to be proud of his crime. He was awarded the death penalty.

Ilm-ud-Din was execution occurred on 31 October 1929. As the time of his execution, he said, 'O people! Bear witness that I killed Rajpal to defend our last Prophet Muhammed S.A.W., and today they are going to hang me. I am sacrificing my life whilst reciting the *kalimah* [testimony of faith].' Allama Iqbal was one of the carriers of the funeral bier. At that moment, Iqbal declared: 'This uneducated young man has surpassed us, the educated ones.'

Ilm-ud-Din has been glorified in Pakistan as a great Islamic hero, a holy warrior, a ghazi, a shaheed, *etc*. There is a mosque commemorating his 'great deed.' In February 2013, the Chief Justice of the Lahore High Court heard arguments on the maintainability of a petition seeking the reopening of an 84-year-old Ilm-ud-Dincase. According to *The Express Tribune* (21 February 2013):

> The petitioner argued that the publisher had insulted the Holy Prophet (peace be upon him) and thus invited his own death. He said Ilmuddin had no personal animosity towards Rajpal, but acted 'out of love for the Holy Prophet (PBUH), like a true Muslim. He asked that Ilmuddin be honoured with state awards and be given a funeral with state protocol.'

In October of the same year, at the two-day celebrations for the eighty-fourth annual Urs of Ghazi Ilm Din Shaheed in the Miani Sahib graveyard, thousands of devotees paid homage to Ghazi Ilm-ud-Din Shaheed. 'Addressing the participants, the scholars vowed to resist all conspiracies being hatched to amend the blasphemy laws under pressure from Washington. They said that no blasphemer could be tolerated in the country created in the name of Islam. They said countless lovers of the Holy Prophet (SAW) like Ghazi Ilm Din Shaheed would emerge if US-slave rulers tried to protect the blasphemers.' (*The News*, 13 October 2013)

The scholars warned that those denying the Islamic punishment of death to the blasphemers were also liable to the same punishment, *The News* reported:

> They accused the rulers and secular elements in the country of conspiring to amend the laws to protect the blasphemers from death. They warned that a countrywide movement would be launched against the rulers if conspiracies continued to amend the blasphemy laws. They demanded death to all those found guilty of committing blasphemy. They also demanded immediate release of Ghazi Mumtaz Qadri who killed former Punjab governor Salman Taseer for allegedly committing blasphemy. They also demanded inclusion of a chapter in the Islamiat syllabus about Ghazi Ilm Din Shaheed, explaining the reason why he killed the blasphemer Rajpal.

The *Rangila Rasul* episode epitomises the fundamental flaw of Orientals: while they are acquainted with the universal ideas and ideals of the Enlightenment—liberty, fairness, tolerance, limited government, *etc.*—they have neither fully imbibed these ideas and ideals nor put them above all other considerations; they have avoided the modern imperative.

In the case of Pakistan, as evident from the above-mentioned reports, even the pretense of clinging to the Enlightenment ideals has been given up over the decades since it became independent. Forget critical inquiry, even music is facing a grave threat over there, with jihadists imposing Islam in its purest form—Freedom of expression in Pakistan is practically dead.

In India, the situation is much better but, as we discussed in the previous chapters, the threats are many and varied, not the least from the political class. The Congress-led government in 2008 introduced an illiberal provision, Section 66A, to the Information Technology Act 2000, which was thankfully struck down by the Supreme Court in 2015. But the worrisome fact is that the government under the Bharatiya Janata Party, which earlier had reservations about Section 66A, also defended the draconian law.

It was the American conservative author William Buckley who said that principles have sharp edges, they cut, they draw blood. The Indian nation—as molded by Gandhi, Nehru, the Congress, and an intellectual class generally sympathetic to them—showed no propensity to stand by the great principles it claimed to espouse and which got enshrined in the Constitution of the Republic. Even in the embryonic stage, the main idea of modernity, of liberty, was compromised.

Many Indians talking about curbs on free speech blame the British Raj for crafting illiberal laws; they bemoan that colonial-era legislation still curtails the freedom of expression; what they don't know, or choose to ignore, is that some illiberality happened because of their own spitefulness. Therefore, Katherine Mayo's *Mother India* remains proscribed in India to this day. Published in 1927, it was critical of Hindu society, religion, and culture; it highlighted, among other things, the maltreatment women and untouchables. The book, which exaggerated some of the shortcomings of India, was fiercely attacked by nationalists. Gandhi called it a 'report of a drain inspector sent out with the one purpose of opening and examining the drains of the country to be reported upon.' At any rate, the British cannot be blamed for the continued ban on *Mother India*. Many other books, like *Old Soldier Sahib* by Private Frank Richards and *The Land of the Lingam* by Arthur Miles, remain proscribed. And, of course, *Rangila Rasul* is still banned. In fact, one particularly legislative provision, Section 295A, intended to restrict freedom of expression, was introduced at the behest of Indians—mainly Muslims but also non-Muslims, including Gandhi. This draconian law was the direct result of the *Rangila Rasul* case, the ensuing Muslim unrest, and the capitulation by most nationalists to the illiberal demands made by Muslims.

The nationalist narrative usually portrays the British as scheming imperialists, unscrupulously deploying divide-and-rule tactics, and generally messing up. But Section 295A, though introduced in the colonial era, came into being because Indians demanded it. Neeta Nair wrote:

> A deputation of leading Muslims called upon the Punjab Governor, Malcolm Hailey, to protest against the High

> Court ruling. The Governor's response, widely published and commented upon, seemed to give a free pass to subsequent Muslim expressions of anger as it sympathised with those Muslims who felt 'justifiably offended' by the pamphlet and felt they had no 'legal weapon by which its repetition could be prevented in the future.' Hailey admitted that the [*Rangila Rasul*] judgment had left the government 'much concerned' for if this type of 'religious controversy could be carried on with impunity' there lay a 'vista of endless trouble before the public.' He also let on that the government had consulted their legal advisers on the appropriateness of undertaking a modification of the law, as Dalip Singh had suggested.

So, the imperial government proposed a Bill to make 'a scurrilous attack upon religion as the substantive matter.' Lajpat Rai called the Bill 'retrograde', yet he found it a 'necessity' given the prevalent 'emergency' situation. This necessary evil, he insisted, should be couched in a language so that '*bona fide* criticism, historical research and all that leads to the interpretation of religious texts in such a way as to lead to progressive reform in social matters will not be affected.' In a similar vein, Jinnah also wanted to 'secure this very important and fundamental principle that those who are engaged in historical works, those who are engaged in the ascertainment of truth and those who are engaged in *bona fide* and honest criticism of a religion shall be protected.'

S. SrinivasaIyengar, leader of the Swarajists in the House, sought 'legislative assistance' from the government to prevent people from 'profaning the sacred name of religion.' Madan Mohan Malaviya, a Hindu nationalist who has recently been honoured by the Narendra Modi government with the highest civilian award, the Bharat Ratna, also supported Section 295A, saying that he was 'less concerned with the facts of the life of any of these glorious men of the world than with the fact that millions of my fellow-men hold each of them in reverence.' So, we got Section 295(A) which says, 'Whoever, with deliberate and malicious intention of outraging the religious feelings of any class…shall be punished…'

There were many misgivings about the proposed law, but on the whole the principle that religious feelings were more important than freedom of expression was accepted; and that acceptance persisted even after the British left India and despite the failure of the law to end the Hindus and Muslims tensions.

India became free, and the Constitution, which took years to be made, was implemented on 26 January 1950. The Constitution had ensured absolute freedom of expression, and this freedom became a fundamental right. Yet, the Jawaharlal Nehru government did not repeal Section 295A, which militated against the spirit of the original Constitution; instead the Constitution was amended and the right to freedom of expression was curtailed.

As we saw earlier, the Indian Constitution imposes 'reasonable restrictions' on the fundamental right to freedom of expression. Reasonable restrictions appended to the freedom of speech and expression in Article 19 (a) pertain to 'the security of the State, friendly relations with foreign States, public order, decency or morality, or in relation to contempt of court, defamation or incitement to an offence.'

Even as these restrictions are an affront to individual liberty and genuine democracy, these are themselves purported to be 'reasonable'. In other words, these can be imposed only if there are *reasonable* grounds for harming national security, jeopardising friendly relations with foreign countries, disturbing public order, offending decency or morality, contemning court, leading to defamation, or occasioning incitement to an offence. Nowhere is it mentioned in the First Amendment that *offending the feelings* or *hurting the sentiments* of somebody can be a ground for curtailment of the freedom of expression.

The grounds restricting the freedom of expression have to be reasonable, and not sentimental, not only because it is the Constitutional position but also because reasons can be objectively debated; sentiments can't be. Unfortunately, our Supreme Court upheld the constitutionality of Section 295A in 1957. Even eminent jurists defend this obnoxious section. In an article in *The Indian Express* (25 June 2006), former attorney general Soli J. Sorabjee wrote: 'The yardstick [to determine whether or not something is scurrilous] is not the standards of hyper-sensitive and volatile minds but those of ordinary persons of normal sensibilities.'

This is an argument to shut the mind of a community or country to questioning, imagination, and innovation. Had Lord Bentick applied the yardstick of the minds 'of ordinary persons of normal sensibilities,' he could not have banned suttee in 1829; in fact, this yardstick would have banished all social reform. Had Galileo been bothered about the sensibilities of ordinary persons, he would never have started his scientific journey. The march of civilisation is predicated upon breaking the chains of ordinariness.

In a nutshell, the Indian nation, the Indian state, the eminent people of India, almost everybody who is somebody in our country has undermined the concepts of individual liberty and freedom of expression, the Supreme Court decision on Section 66A notwithstanding. Free speech has been downgraded considerably over the decades because of hurt feelings, political expedience, or downright mischief. And few are bothered.

Charlie Hebdo massacre

Contrast this situation with the reaction of almost the entire Western world to attack on *Charlie Hebdo*, a Paris-based French satirical weekly magazine whose defining feature is irreverence. Secular, atheistic, and leftwing, it published stories, cartoons, polemics, and jokes which offended every possible sensibility—rightwing, nationalist, Christian, Judaic, and, most spectacularly, Islamic. For the last one, the magazine had to pay a heavy price.

On 7 January 2015, two Muslim terrorists forced their way into the headquarters of the magazine and fired indiscriminately, leaving behind a dozen people and wounding eleven. The jihadists kept shouting *Allahu Akbar*, along with 'the Prophet is avenged.'

The condemnation of the outrage was universal; except a few deranged, multiculturalism-infested intellectuals who talked about 'respect' for other religions and cultures, the entire Western world stood united against the attack on its most cherished ideal—liberty. On 11 January, BBC reported:

> More than three million people have taken part in unity marches across France after 17 people died during three days of deadly attacks in Paris. Up to 1.6 million are estimated to have taken to the streets of the French capital. More than 40 world leaders joined the start of the Paris march, linking arms in an act of solidarity.

The leaders included British Prime Minister David Cameron, German Chancellor Angela Merkel, Israeli Prime Minister Benjamin Netanyahu, Palestinian President Mahmoud Abbas, Malian President Ibrahim Boubacar Keita, EU President Donald Tusk, and Jordan's King Abdullah

II. 'Paris is the capital of the world today,' French leader Francois Hollande said (US President Barack Obama was conspicuous by his absence, which is attributed to his doubts about absolute freedom of expression).

'Je suis Charlie' (French for 'I am Charlie') was quickly adopted as a slogan by the supporters of freedom of expression. Of course, multicultural bigots also came up with 'Je Ne Suis Pas Charlie' ('I am not Charlie'), but 'Je suis Charlie' was the dominant theme.

What was heartening to see was that all ideological differences were forgotten on the issue of freedom; the socialist Hollande joined hands with the Conservative Cameron to defend the most cherished ideal of the Western civilisation; similarly, activists and votaries of various persuasions buried their differences for the common cause.

While Orientals tolerate the gradual erosion of the freedom of expression, Westerners make it clear that liberty is not negotiable. This makes the West superior to the East.

Chapter 24

Internet censorship: A growing menace

Internet censorship is rampant in India. It increased when the Congress-led government in New Delhi (2004-14), facing trenchant criticism in cyberspace because of its corruption and misrule, was keen to check adverse comment. Then there were other organisations, including political parties like the Shiv Sena, which were unwilling to take any censure in their stride. While the judiciary has mostly helped the cause of freedom, its record has not been unblemished. A high court judge asked social networking sites and search engines to 'have a stringent check. Otherwise, like in China, we may pass orders banning all such websites.'

The Information Technology Act 2000(ITA, 2000) was enacted citing a resolution A/RES/51/162, dated 30 January 1997, by the General Assembly of the United Nations. The UN resolution 'adopted the Model Law on Electronic Commerce adopted by the United Nations Commission on International Trade Law', according to a government website. This resolution had recommended, 'inter alia, that all States give favourable consideration to the said Model Law when they enact or revise their laws, in view of the need for uniformity of the law applicable to alternatives to paper-cased methods of communication and storage of information.' Further, 'it is considered necessary to give effect to the said resolution and to promote efficient delivery of Government services by means of reliable electronic records.'

According to the government, this was an:

> Act to provide legal recognition for transactions carried out by means of electronic data interchange and other means of electronic communication, commonly referred to as 'electronic commerce', which involve the use of alternatives to paper-based methods of communication and storage of information, to facilitate electronic filing of documents with the government agencies and further to amend the Indian Penal Code, the Indian Evidence Act 1872, the Bankers' Books Evidence Act 1891, and the Reserve Bank of India Act 1934, and for matters connected therewith or incidental thereto.

The notorious section

When the Congress-led government in New Delhi started undoing economic reforms, implementing mindlessly populist schemes, indulging in shameless corruption, and appeasing Muslims, there was a backlash on social media. The mainstream media was duly tamed. The question was: what to do with social media?

Therefore, rattled by incessant denunciation on the net, in 2008, the government amended the Information Technology Act 2000, and introduced the notorious Section 66A. The Amendment has severely curtailed the freedom of expression. The Open Net Initiative (ONI), an international project to monitor and report on Internet filtering and surveillance practices by nations, said in 2011 that India was engaged in 'selective' Internet filtering in the political, conflict/security, social, and Internet tools areas. According to ONI, India is a 'stable democracy with a strong tradition of press freedom, [but the country] nevertheless continues its regime of Internet filtering.' In March 2012, Reporters Without Borders put India in its list of 'countries under surveillance.'

In its 2012 report, Freedom House categorised India as 'partly free.' Freedom House is a prestigious American non-governmental organisation that conducts research and advocacy on democracy, political freedom, and human rights. On a scale from 0 (most free) to 100 (least free), India had a score of 39. In 2011, the score was 36,which means that considerable freedom was eroded in a year.

This was not surprising because the government in April 2011, instituted Information Technology (Intermediary Guidelines) Rules, which imposed strict conditions on intermediaries such as Internet Service Providers (ISPs) and social networking sites; they were supposed to remove 'offensive' content within thirty-six hours on individual complaints. The rules made the already draconian provisions of the Information Technology Act 2008 even more stringent. Anything that was deemed 'disparaging', 'harmful', 'blasphemous', 'pornographic', encouraging gambling, infringing on proprietary rights or threatening 'the unity, integrity, defense, security or sovereignty of India, friendly relations with foreign states or public order,' was brought under the ambit of the 2011 rules. The vagueness of rules augmented the sphere of discretion of law-enforcement agencies.

Goebbels at odds with Goering?

In December 2011, the Minister of Communications Kapil Sibal openly started talking about prescreening Internet content. His officials were pressuring ISPs and social media sites, including Google and Facebook, to 'prescreen user content from India and to remove disparaging, inflammatory or defamatory content before it goes online.' Senior executives at these companies were in regular touch with Sibal's ministry. Sibal reportedly urged these companies 'to use human beings to screen content, not technology'.

At a press conference he said, 'We have to take care of the sensibilities of our people.' By which he meant his own party's sensibilities, for Sonia Gandhi and her son Rahul, along with other Congress grandees like Digvijay Singh, were regularly lambasted and lampooned on the net. Sibal, however, provided the gloss of culture to his government's nefarious designs: 'Cultural ethos is very important to us.' A Goebbels disagreeing with Goering!

Chapter 25

Global threats to liberty

For centuries, plunderers, tyrants, slavers, and other enemies of peace and liberty carried out pillage by brutal force; they relied on the principle that might is right. Those were the times when life was often poor, nasty, brutish, and short.

Thankfully, those times are behind us—at any rate, behind most of us. There are widely, almost universally, accepted ideas, values, norms, and conventions about the inviolability of human life, inalienable rights of men and women, human dignity, and so on. There is, however, no call to become complacent because the enemies of freedom are still active. They no longer come with marauding armies and lethal weaponry; they no longer massacre, rape, and build towers of human skulls; they are not in the likeness of a Genghis Khan or a Timur; they are suave glib talkers who often espouse fashionable causes. But make no mistake about it: the enemies of liberty have not become extinct.

And they come in various guises. When curbing economic freedoms, they champion the causes of poverty alleviation, effective corporate social responsibility, stringer regulations, *etc*. When attacking the freedom of expression, they take recourse to otherwise laudable concepts like public morality, national security, and decency. The consequences of their actions, however, are the same: further shrinking of the sphere of liberty.

OIC undermines liberty

The recent international threats of censorship have come from the Organisation of Islamic Countries (OIC) and the ostensibly innocuous efforts of an almost one-and-a-half-century-old organisation under the United Nations. Let us begin with the UN body.

The International Telecommunication Union (ITU), set up as the International Telegraph Union in 1865, has the mandate to promote information and communication technologies. Headquartered in Geneva, Switzerland, the ITU looks into issues related to coordination in telecom, radio spectrum use, and the like. Almost all countries in the world are members of the ITU; other members include equipment manufacturers, funding bodies and international and regional telecom organisations.

In December 2012 in Dubai, eighty-nine ITU member countries signed a global treaty on telecom regulations which was opposed by, among others, the US, other developed countries, and India. Mohamed al-Ghanim, chairman of the World Conference on International Telecommunication (WICT-12), organised by the ITU, hoped that other countries would follow suit and sign the treaty.

On the face of it, the WICT-12 objectives were unexceptional, even agreeable. ITU Secretary General Hamadoun Toure said, 'This conference was not about the Internet control or Internet governance and indeed there are no provisions on the internet.'

The resolution on the internet was non-binding. It recognised, among other things, that 'all governments should have an equal role and responsibility for international Internet governance and for ensuring the stability, security and continuity of the existing internet and its future development and of the future internet.' Further, Toure said that the preamble contains a special article in which member states 'affirm their commitment to implement these regulations in a manner that respects and upholds their human rights obligations.'

The treaty said:

> New provisions in the text place special emphasis on future efforts to assist developing countries, on promoting accessibility to persons with disabilities, and on asserting all peoples' right to freedom of expression over ICT [information and communications technology] communication networks.

Further it said:

> Other pioneering new provisions include a resolution to create a single, globally harmonised number for access to emergency services, new text mandating greater transparency in the prices set for mobile roaming, and new provisions to improve the energy efficiency of ICT networks and help combat e-waste.

Toure is right insofar as his contention that WICT-12 was not about Internet control is concerned. The treaty does not contain anything that seeks to control or censor cyberspace. But the question is: why was the Dubai meeting held in the first place? The internet has been spreading and growing around the world on its own steam.

UAE shows the path

The second concern arises from the venue of the meeting and the character of the hosts. Steven Strauss, Advanced Leadership Fellow at Harvard University, wrote for the *Huffington Post* just a month before the meeting that 'the UAE issued by decree (without public debate, comment periods, or other democratic niceties) a new law making it a crime to deride, insult, mock or criticise, by using the internet, the leaders of the UAE.' The biggest backers of the WICT-12 were China, Russia, and the Muslim world; all of them had, and continue to have, issues with the concept of freedom of expression.

It is well known that China has been suppressing the views of dissenters, imprisoning human rights activists, and pressuring Internet service providers. In Russia, Vladimir Putin is trying to control the internet. Muslims all over the world want anything less than laudatory about their religion or the Prophet to be proscribed.

Thanks to Muslims' immense petro-wealth and influence and the liberals' predilection for what they term multiculturalism, there are already a few international norms curtailing the freedom of expression in matters pertaining to Islam. The fact that the United Nations—along with many other international organisations—has become a platform for multiculturalism, political correctness, and other anti-Enlightenment pathologies has only exacerbated the situation.

...and others follow

In April 1999, at the behest of the OIC, Pakistan brought before the United Nations Commission on Human Rights a resolution called Defamation of Islam. It urged

> all States, within their national legal framework, in conformity with international human rights instruments to take all appropriate measures to combat hatred, discrimination, intolerance and acts of violence, intimidation and coercion motivated by religious intolerance, including attacks on religious places, and to encourage understanding, tolerance and respect in matters relating to freedom of religion or belief.

The resolution was adopted by the Commission.

Many more resolutions were passed by the UNHRC. The 2010 resolution, called Combating Defamation of Religions, specifically expressed 'deep concern... that Islam is frequently and wrongly associated with human rights violations and terrorism and in this regard regrets the laws or administrative measures specifically designed to control and monitor the Muslim minorities, thereby stigmatising them and legitimising the discrimination they experience.'

Interestingly, while the UNHRC has been urging the non-Muslim world to shed 'Islamophobia', it has been largely silent over the marginalisation of and discrimination against non-Muslims in Islamic countries and the growing hard-line Islamism all over the world. In Saudi Arabia, for instance, non-Muslims cannot worship, celebrate their festivals, or even name their children as Ram and Benjamin.

Unfortunately, the OIC's nefarious efforts have got some support from US President Barack Obama. At the UN in September 2012, Obama said: 'The future must not belong to those who slander the prophet of Islam.' In the US, which has a strong conservative and libertarian establishment, censorship efforts began before Obama's presidency. Intellectual Conservative editor Rachel Alexander wrote in an article:

> The move towards censorship in the US started under the second Bush administration. In 2008, the Department of Homeland Security issued a memo containing recommendations from

> Muslim organisations that instruct Americans to avoid using words like 'jihadist', 'Islamic terrorist', 'Islamist', and 'holy warrior.' When referring to Muslims, words like 'mainstream','ordinary', and 'traditional' should be used instead of terms like 'moderate'. The 'War on Terror' is to be rephrased as 'a global challenge, which transcends geography, culture, and religion.'[9]

In 2012, she wrote:

> the FBI was ordered by the Obama administration to purge language from its manuals, and subsequently removed more than 700 documents and 300 presentations from training materials. All federal law enforcement agencies were ordered to eliminate the words 'Islamic terror' from their training manuals. The Pentagon's Quadrennial Defense Review and the Quadrennial Homeland Security Review were revised to eliminate the words 'Muslim' and 'Islam'. Mentions of al Qaeda were replaced with 'global violent extremism.'

In Eurabia

The situation in Europe is even worse. According to the American author and feminist psychologist Phyllis Chesler, 'Europe, once the birthplace of freedom, is fast becoming its graveyard.' Expressing unconventional views has been met with violence by Muslims; worse, governments have sought to suppress free speech. In 2004 in Holland, journalist and filmmaker Theo Van Gogh was murdered by Muslim fanatics. His collaborator and legislator, Ayaan Hirsi Ali, who is known for her critical views on Islam, had to go into hiding. In 2009, the Dutch politician Geert Wilders faced a trial because of for his uncharitable remarks about Islam.

Elisabeth Sabaditsch-Wolff, a free speech activist in Austria, was charged in 2010 with 'denigration of religious beliefs of a legally recognised religion.' In the same year, the American author Bruce Bawer and his Norwegian colleagues had a brush with the law; they were accused

9 See www.townhall.com

of 'racism' and 'Islamophobia'. Unsurprisingly, the champions of liberty dread the prospects of Eurabia, the growing Islamisation of Europe.

There are many more instances of (often successful) attempts to suppress free speech in Europe. Whether it is Europe, the US, or any other place, the enemies of the freedom of expression sugarcoat their demands with nice terms like 'peaceful coexistence' and 'diversity'. As I mentioned in the beginning of this chapter, the enemies of liberty in our time are sophisticated people. Multiculturalism is their armour, political correctness is their weapon, and postmodern jargon is their camouflage.

Chapter 26

There no such thing as hate speech

The issue of hate speech does crop up frequently in India and elsewhere. Politicians, and often other public figures, all over the world are accused of making hate speech. In general, any nasty comment—actually, any remark—that somebody does not like is called'hate speech.' Demands are made to criminalise something as nebulous as 'hate speech.'

Before proceeding to establish my assertion—there is no such thing as hate speech—I would like to discuss the concept of hate crime. Merriam-Webster defines 'hate crime' as 'any of various crimes (as assault or defacement of property) when motivated by hostility to the victim as a member of a group (as one based on colour, creed, gender, or sexual orientation).' The US Congress describes a hate crime as 'a criminal offense against a person or property motivated in whole or in part by an offender's bias against a race, religion, disability, ethnic origin or sexual orientation.' Hate itself is not a crime—and the Federal Bureau of Investigation of the US is mindful of protecting freedom of speech and other civil liberties, says the FBI website.

Two points need to be made here. First, hate speech should not be confused with hate crime; the former, however offensive and repulsive be its content, is still speech, a form of expression, and any form of expression is and should be protected in a liberal democracy. The latter, on the other hand, is crime, and should be dealt with accordingly.

Second, hate is not and cannot be a crime in a democracy. On the face of it, this sounds paradoxical. For doesn't the Preamble of the Constitution of India, the world's largest democracy, talk about the resolve 'to secure'—apart from justice, liberty, and equality—fraternity? How fraternity can be secured without rooting out, or at least checking, hate?

But this line of thinking is fallacious and fraught with the possibility of bolstering totalitarian tendencies; for hate, like love, lies within an individual's heart and mind; and any move to regulate the hearts and minds of citizens is tantamount to thought control—the defining feature of totalitarianism. The purpose of legislation in a liberal polity is to legislate *between individuals*, to regulate inter-individual conduct and *not intra-individual* dynamics. Criminalising hate would amount to defining thought crime—another totalitarian tendency. Thankfully, the anti-totalitarian streak is implicit in the Preamble, inasmuch as it describes fraternity as 'assuring the dignity of the individual.' It is obvious, then, that the dignity of the individual will be destroyed if the state decides to indulge in thoughtcontrol, an endeavour that would necessitate intrusion into the most sacred spaces of the individual. Such fundamental rights as freedom of speech and expression (Article 19) and freedom of conscience (Article 25), enshrined in the Constitution, shield these spaces.

Besides, the Preamble of the Indian Constitution, like the Directive Principles of State Policy, is non-justiciable. Therefore, fraternity cannot be legislated; similarly, the government cannot execute and the courts cannot adjudicate all the cherished goals of the Constitution. The three organs of the state—with the paraphernalia of laws, rules, and regulations—can help create an environment conducive for a liberal, fair, just, and peaceable existence. In short, an efficacious state is the necessary but not the sufficient condition for make a country a better place.

If we accept that hate cannot be a crime, we also have to accept that, as a natural corollary, hate speech also cannot be a crime. But, it will be asked, what about the reprehensible comments made by politicians and others? Sample the following statements made by Indian politicians in 2014:

(a) People should vote for *Ramzade* (children of Ram) and not *Haramzade* (bastards)—Federal Minister Sadhvi Niranjan Jyoti in the Narendra Modi government.

(b) If you keep petrol and fire together then it will burn. There should be a law to ensure that there should be no *nangapan* (nudity). Those who wear less clothes should also be banned. Fashion and nudity are responsible for the current situation in India. And in rural India, girls don't go searching out for boyfriends. I support death penalty for the Delhi rapists but there should also be a law that women should not wear less clothes and roam around with boys who are not their relatives. What is the need for roaming at night with men who are not relatives? This should be stopped—Samajwadi (Socialist) Party leader Abu Azmi.

(c) If you insult the mothers and daughters of Trinamool workers, then I won't spare you. I will let loose my boys in your homes and they will commit rape. I will teach each of you a lesson—Tapas Pal, popular Bengali actor and Trinamool Congress MP.

(d) You Hindus are 100 crore (one billion) and we Muslims are 25 crore (250 million). Just remove police for fifteen minutes and we will show you who is more powerful—Akbaruddin Owaisi, prominent Muslim Legislator in the southern state of Andhra Pradesh (2013).

(e) The concept of four wives and forty children just won't work in India but it is high time that every Hindu woman must produce at least four children to protect the Hindu religion—Sakshi Maharaj, BJP MP from Unnao, UP (2015).

These are some of the more shameful remarks made by Indian politicians. The question is: should the law permit such remarks? The answer is a big 'yes.' The only caveat is that the speech should not trigger an immediate violent action.

In fact, *allowing* the so-called hate speech will have a salutary effect in a democracy. This will enhance transparency in democracy. The electorate will know what disdain Owaisi harbours for the Hindus, his party's professions for plurality, diversity, and peaceful coexistence notwithstanding. Similarly, the prospective voters of Sakshi Maharaj will get an idea about his views on women, that they are little better than baby-making machines.

We shall scrutinise the concept of hate speech as commonly understood. Collins Dictionary defines 'hate speech' as 'speech disparaging a racial, sexual, or ethnic group or a member of such a group.' Dictionary. com describes it as 'speech that attacks, threatens, or insults a person or group on the basis of national origin, ethnicity, color, religion, gender, gender identity, sexual orientation, or disability.'

There are three features of the notion of hate speech: first, it is directed at a collectivity or a member of a collectivity; second, the collectivity is birth-based, and that includes sexual orientation with the assumption it is innate rather than acquired; and, third, it is possible to disparage, attack, threaten, or insult a group by way of expression, be it a newspaper article, a lecture, a song, a novel, or a movie.

There are two main problems with the notion. The first one relates to the first two features: overemphasis on the importance of birth-based collectivities. This is unfortunate and anachronistic, for business, commerce, migration, and globalisation have shrunk the world and brought the people of various civilisations, cultures, races, and faiths together. At a time when people are shedding their prejudices and phobias about other nationalities, races, religions, *etc.*, politicians and intellectuals are exacerbating the differences and building new walls between different collectivities.

The second, and graver, problem with the notion of hate speech pertains to the third feature: the very possibility of disparagement, attack, threat, or insult to a group by free speech. My contention is that it is impossible to disparage, attack, *etc.*, a group by way of words or any other form of human expression. One reason that it is impossible to malign a collectivity or community in a scholarly or any other fashion in this day and age is that nobody has an absolute control over knowledge and information. In ancient and medieval times, monks in Europe and Brahmins in India had a hold over almost all the institutions of imparting knowledge. In India, there was a large section of the society, called Shudras, who were doctrinally barred from receiving canonical education, the only kind of education available.

Such a situation, thankfully, does not prevail in the world today. There are so many and so varied sources of information and means of disseminating information that today it is not possible to keep spreading lies, calumny, and canards against any group—unless, of course, it is a gang of criminals.

We need to remember that within every belief system if there are fringe elements, there are also reasonable thinkers who debunk the extremist and violent doctrines—and the reasonable voices are often the dominant ones. Generally, there is regard for common decencies. For instance, former journalist and Federal Minister Arun Shourie, a most prominent rightwing ideologue, slammed anti-Christian utterances of Hindu militants in 2015. Similarly, in the wake of the massacre of nine black parishioners in a Charleston church by a 21-year-old racist, Dylann Roof, all mainstream rightists condemned the outrage.

Therefore, as the third American president, Thomas Jefferson (1801-1809), said in his First Inaugural Address, 'error of opinion may be tolerated where reason is left free to combat it.'

The law should come into force only when speech immediately triggers harm, or when the speech-maker takes full responsibility of the instigation, as was the case with the son-of-the-soil Maharashtra Leader Raj Thackeray. He made hateful remarks about the Hindi-speaking migrants to Maharashtra, leading to violent activities by his followers. It was a clear case of hate crime, which has not been punished till date, despite audio-visual evidence and the boastful admissions of the crimes both by the speech-makers and hooligans. It is a topsy-turvy world that we, the people of India, live in: all efforts are made criminalise freedom of expression, whereas as blatant criminal activities go unpunished.

This brings us to the final point: in the case of speech, or any other form of expression, criminality should be linked to its effect rather than its content, more so because in such matters cure is better than prevention. The situation is similar to the regulation in the economy: ideally, regulation should be light andseek very fewcompliances, but fraud should be swiftly, efficaciously, and severely punished, thus instilling the fear of the law in the hearts of wrongdoers. When economic offenders know that the chances of getting caught are high, they are effectively deterred. The high probability of the law catching up with the wrongdoer works as an effective deterrence, strict compliances don't. It is impossible to deter fraudsters by trying to preclude racket, for they are very ingenious; but it is possible to do so by ensuring punishment.

Similarly, it would be possible to bring down hate crime if the potential perpetrators know that violent consequences would result in prosecution. In a nutshell, there is no such thing as hate speech; there is only speech, which ought to be free. Sometimes, a speech does spread hatred; if the hatred immediately results in violence, it is a crime, a hate crime, and should be penalised in proportion to the severity of the crime; if not, the worst that can be said about it is that it was in bad taste, deserving condemnation and nothing more.

About The Author

Ravi Shanker Kapoor holds a B.A. Mathematics (Honours) degree from Hansraj College, Delhi University. As a journalist for over 25 years he has been associated with several newspapers such as The Financial Express and The Asian Age, and as a freelancer, he has also contributed to Business Standard, The Wall Street Journal and The Indian Express, among others. Kapoor has also authored More Equal Than Others: A Study of the Indian Left (2000), a book about the huge intellectual influence communists enjoy, even if their influence is greatly disproportionate to their political strength. His second book, Failing the Promise: Irrelevance of the Vajpayee Government (2003), was about the failure of the BJP to provide a viable, rightwing alternative. The third one, How India's Intellectuals Spread Lies (2007), exposed luminaries like Jawaharlal Nehru, Arundhati Roy, Khushwant Singh, Kuldip Nayar and Mani Shankar Aiyar. He depicted them as people who mindlessly parrot the lies of communism. These books were published by Vision Books.

Currently, he edits www.thehinduchronicle.com

www.ingramcontent.com/pod-product-compliance
Ingram Content Group UK Ltd.
Pitfield, Milton Keynes, MK11 3LW, UK
UKHW041313190726
13845UKWH00025B/243

9 789386 432728